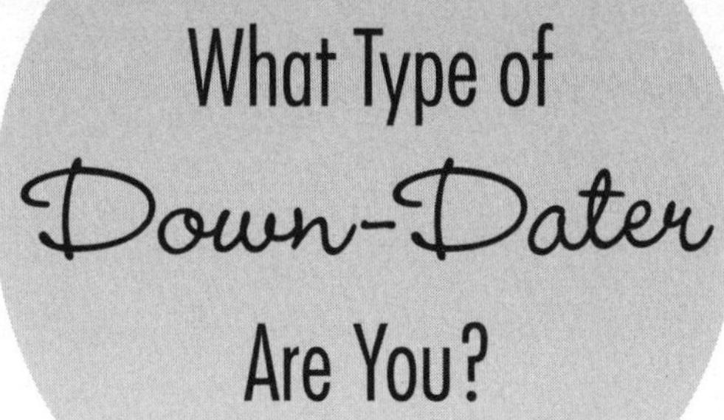

# What Type of Down-Dater Are You?

**Mommy Dearest.** You chide him when he's late, you remind him to eat his vegetables, and you forbid him from blowing all his money on beer until he gets himself a job. Face it—you don't have a boyfriend, you have a teenage son.

**Ms. "I Love Him for What He Is, Not What He Does" (also goes by "The Denial Artist").** If you're an architect and he's the weekend manager at Pizza Hut, this might make for a bit of head-butting.

**The Too-Busy Bessie.** Breaking up with your unworthy boyfriend and finding a man who deserves you isn't an activity you can program into your PDA. It's something that you need to do right away—no matter how busy you are.

**The "But He's Changing" Girl.** If your boyfriend wasn't the man you wanted him to be when you met—emotionally, financially, intellectually, or in any other way—chances are he never will be.

**The "I Just Bought a Book Called *Dating Up*" Woman.** Why should you take my word for it? Because I've tried these techniques and shared them with the frustrated women I know, and they actually work. In other words, I'm not only the Dating Up president. I'm also a client.

# DATING UP

## Dump the Schlump and Find a Quality Man

J. Courtney Sullivan

WARNER BOOKS

NEW YORK BOSTON

While this book is a work of nonfiction, the identities of some of the persons referred to and certain details about them have been modified.



Warner Books
Hachette Book Group USA
1271 Avenue of the Americas
New York, NY 10020

Visit our Web site at www.HachetteBookGroupUSA.com

Printed in the United States of America

First Edition: February 2007
10 9 8 7 6 5 4 3 2 1



Library of Congress Cataloging-in-Publication Data
Sullivan, J. Courtney
Dating up : dump the schlump and find a quality man / J. Courtney Sullivan. —
1st ed.
p. cm.
ISBN-13: 978-0-446-69760-6
ISBN-10: 0-446-69760-5
1. Dating (Social customs). 2. Mate selection. I. Title.
HQ801.S923 2007
646.7'7082—dc22
2006016879

*Cover design by Claire Brown*
*Interior design and page composition by rlf design*

*For my parents, who have proven that great*

*and lasting love still exists.*

*And for my sister Caroline,*

*who never settles for less than she deserves.*

# Acknowledgments

Thank you to the brave men who shared their stories, and surprised me with their wisdom and honesty.

Thank you to the women who have inspired and impressed me all along, especially Lauren Semino, Maxine Rodburg, Lucie Prinz, Laura Smith, Aliya Niazi, Michelle Burke, Laura Bonner, Olessa Pindak, Erin Quinn, Patty Tortolani, and the GSG.

Thanks to my extended family for the love, stories, and advice; to Tricia Sweeney for the recipes; to Josh Friedman for the endless wisdom and occasional gossip; and to Colin Fox, my partner in crime, who has proven that the book really works.

A thousand *thank-yous* to my magnificent agent, Brettne Bloom; my brilliant editor, Karen Kosztolnyik; the fabulous Elly Weisenberg, and all the wonderful people at Warner Books.

And special thanks to Karin Kringen, who saw me through many a schlump, and helped create the concept for *Dating Up* in that birthplace of all great ideas, the Banana Republic dressing room.

# Contents

Introduction 1

One: **Getting Ready** 21

Two: **Go Out and Find Him** 83

Three: **The First Date** 125

Four: **Going the Distance** 149

Five: **Marrying Up** 231

**The Ten Tenets of Dating Up** 255

About the Author 260

# Dating Up

# Introduction

**Lo-ser** \ *lü-z&r* \ *n:* **1** : One that loses especially consistently **2** : One who is incompetent or unable to succeed; *also* : something doomed to fail or disappoint.

**Down-dater** \ *doun-'dater* \ *n:* A woman of good character, sound mind, solid education, and great ambition, who cannot seem to tear herself apart from starving artists, men with money but no hearts, and all other classes of loser.

So you're a down-dater. You meet unimpressive guys who are beneath you, and you cling to them for dear life, while turning a blind eye to all the fabulous, intelligent, wealthy men of the world.

Welcome to the club.

By the time my best friends and I left Smith College in

2003, we had graduated with honors, gotten jobs in the fields and cities of our choice, and begun thinking about how to invest for the future. We had also collectively dated an impressive string of losers including "Brooklyn Ben," a twenty-nine-year-old aspiring rock star who carried a cloth Smurf wallet with a Velcro clasp; "Little Piggy," the unusually short heir to a sausage fortune, who threw away his parents' money on long weekends in Vegas and didn't own a single book; "The Stripper's Assistant," a used-car salesman with a kid, who accompanied his best friend—a male stripper in army paint—to gigs as a bodyguard; "Virgin Atlantic," an unpublished British poet who still lived with his mom and was more talk than action; "Brad with the Broken Nose," a construction worker with a propensity for barroom brawls; and "Eddie the Drug Dealer"—no explanation needed.

Starving artists, social miscreants, or hell, any guy living slightly above the poverty line were all the rage back in college, when our greatest expense was Corona with lime. But now we're thinking ahead, realizing that our choice of partners will determine our lifelong social and economic happiness, and that a guy's cute spiky hair or vintage LP collection will take a girl only so far. We're determining what's most important. For some of us, it's the ability to quit our job and stay home with our kids one day. For others, it's a husband who works as hard as we do and has earning potential that's equal to or greater than our own. And for others still, it's a four-bedroom house in Bridgehampton with an ocean view. Whatever the reason, suddenly that old phrase of Mom's—"It's just as easy to fall in love with a rich man as it is to fall in love with a poor man"—doesn't seem so prehistoric after all.

I'm not suggesting that we run out and get boob jobs, or that we forget about chemistry and marry the nearest millionaire on a ventilator. I didn't go to Gloria Steinem's alma mater for four years to write a book about gold digging. *Dating Up* is about more than just money. It's about finding a man who is your intellectual equal and wants the same things out of life you do—success, happiness, stability, and financial security. Marrying for money alone won't lead to a life of wedded bliss, but it's time that women stop feeling bad about admitting that money matters. We deserve to be challenged, excited, and (yes, I'll admit it) supported—financially and otherwise—by the men in our lives. Acknowledging that fact doesn't diminish our independence. It just makes us aware of what we need from a partner and gets us that much closer to finding Mr. Right (and ditching Mr. Are-You-Kidding-Me).

Men of quality are everywhere. And the tools for finding and keeping one are only slightly different from the tools you needed to get that dude with the earring who just asked if he could borrow ten bucks for cab fare. These men want all the things in a mate that other men want, plus an added element of refinement and worldliness. They need partners who are comfortable around wealth, who carry themselves with confidence, who have seen the world, and know their Picasso from their Pollock, their Dostoevsky from their Dominick Dunne.

In these pages, you will learn how to locate and keep a quality wealthy man. From looking your best, to educating yourself about wine, art, travel, and literature; from striking up a conversation at the gym or an Ivy League club, to meeting his mother and making her love you, I have gathered tips and tricks from quality men and the women they marry, and put all of them to the test, to make sure that I'm giving you the information you need.

Marrying the right kind of man is about staying true to who you are, while enhancing yourself. It's about knowing the places to meet great men and getting ready to snag one once you do. It's not about being a gold digger or settling for money over love. It's about finding the whole package and knowing how to make it yours.

In my preliminary research for this book, I interviewed dozens of successful, smart, and otherwise happy women, who keep falling into one unsuccessful, unwise, unhappy relationship after another. Most of them know what they're doing to sabotage their own love lives, but feel that eventually they'll grow out of it. Wrong. Dating is like dieting—you can't just say "I'm dying to lose weight, so I think I'll eat whatever I want and hope that I drop fifteen pounds." Likewise, you can't keep dating losers and expect to wake up next to Prince Charming one of these days. You need a strategy, and that's where *Dating Up* comes in.

Before we move on to dating up, let's explore why we down-date in the first place and how to identify the losers to whom we tend to give our hearts. (Isn't overanalyzing fun? If it had been a varsity sport in high school, I would have been captain of the team.) Here are the ten most common types of down-dater. Recognize yourself? If so, read on.

1. **Mommy Dearest.** Even though he's unemployed and you work full-time, he can't seem to remember to wash his dirty socks—but you can. Even though you have a busy social calendar, you constantly remind him of job interviews, doctor's appointments, and family birthdays

that have slipped his mind. You chide him when he's late, you remind him to eat his vegetables, and you forbid him from blowing all his money on beer until he gets himself a job. Face it: you don't have a boyfriend, you have a teenage son. It's easy to get lured into this particular trap, because a lot of us confuse feelings of romance with the urge to nurture. But what's going to happen when you actually have children? Do you want to be taking care of him then? The man you end up with should be your equal. Yes, you should take care of each other in small ways, but first it's important to know that you both can tie your own shoelaces. Your attention to detail and urge to be the boss will serve you better at work than in a romantic relationship. If you just can't bear the thought of losing a warm body in the bed at night, and an expectant "feed me" look each time you walk through the door, dump the toddler-man and get a golden retriever.

2. **The Mother-Seeker.** The overly mothering girlfriend has been around for centuries, but throughout the past few decades, an increase in the number of women in the workplace has spawned a new breed of overly mothering men. These guys cook all your meals, clean up after you, and generally make sure your life runs smoothly while you're out there living it. They are usually unemployed, or work one hour for every ten that you log in. Meanwhile, you grow so comfortable with having everything done for you that you never pause to think about whether or not you actually like the guy, or whether he's your intellectual equal (probably not if he's doing a

handyman's job for free). Leaky faucet? Call your boyfriend. New couch needs to be delivered between noon and three? Call your boyfriend. Hospital corners on the sheets were a little sloppy this morning? Call your boyfriend. All of the above sound like you? Dump your boyfriend, and call a housekeeping service.

3. **Ms. "I Love Him for Who He Is, Not What He Does" (also goes by "The Denial Artist").** We've all been there. Maybe for just one date, maybe for a month or two, or in the case of most women I know (and okay, me too) for a number of years. You meet a guy and feel an instant connection—he's so smart, so funny, so well read, so interesting. And far less pretentious than all the guys you were with in college. The only problem is that he never went to college (look out for phrases like, "Why would I pay a hundred grand for a piece of paper?" or "You think just because you spent four years staring at a blackboard, it means you're smart?") and he makes next-to-nothing. Just remember that for all the time you spend trying to convince your friends and your mother that money and job status aren't important, you are probably trying just as hard to convince yourself. Not that you should turn down a date with someone because he isn't a Rockefeller, but it's essential to admit that money matters in relationships. Somewhere between our grandmothers, who stayed home and expected a man to provide, and ourselves, many of whom feel disempowered if a man so much as opens a door for us, the message about money and relationships got fuzzy. It went from "Money is everything" to "If I think money

matters, I must be a heartless ice queen who can't take care of herself." Earning power matters in a mate—and each of us can decide exactly how much of it we need to feel comfortable. You and your future husband will make every financial decision together—the neighborhood you live in, the social circle you choose, the vacations you take, the way you educate your children, and more. If you're an architect and he's the weekend manager at Pizza Hut, this might make for a bit of head-butting. Think of it like *Titanic*—a beautiful love story about the cruelty of class distinctions, but face it: if Leonardo hadn't gone down with the ship, that relationship never would have made it onto dry land.

4. **The Money Maniac.** Though it's important to feel financially comfortable in a relationship, money isn't everything. I once had a friend who spoke about her boyfriend constantly. Well, not him exactly, but his car (a Bentley), his vacation homes (Monte Carlo and Corfu), his credit card (a black AmEx that he let her take for a spin on Rodeo Drive every weekend), and his expense account (a limitless perk of his high-paying consultant job). She never once mentioned his interests, his friends, or his personality. When I asked her what they had in common, she said it was simple—"He likes making money, and I like spending it." Have we learned nothing from Donald Trump's ex-wives? You need more than financial freedom to make a relationship work. Take a hint from the grand master of marrying-for-money: Jane Austen. Those who married just for the big house and the title (see Charlotte Lucas in *Pride and*

*Prejudice*) always ended up miserable and penniless (suckahs!). Those who chose the men they loved, who incidentally were pretty well-off (see the amazing Elizabeth Bennet) lived happily ever after.

5. **The "I'm Not Worthy" Worrier.** For six months, my friend George—a surgeon with JFK Junior good looks—was obsessed with a girl in his running club. "She's gorgeous," he said. "I heard her laugh today and it was so cute. You should have seen her kick all the other girls' asses. She runs a seven-minute mile." When the gushing started bordering on nausea, I suggested that he do the obvious: ask Ms. Perfect out. George told me that he already had, several times, but again and again she turned him down. I wondered if she was married, blind, insane, or all three, but he said no—"just not interested." A few weeks later, over beers with their entire club, George tried again, and this time, fueled by the truth serum that is Amstel Light, she told him that his job, his Harvard medical degree, and his big blue eyes intimidated her. "Guys like you make me nervous," she said. "There's just too much pressure." Now this one really annoys me, because of the number of women who are always complaining that there are no good men out there. In reality, men with charm, brains, and manners are everywhere, but we seem to keep choosing their obnoxious, ill-bred counterparts over them. What are we afraid of? Perhaps "the Little Runner That Could" hit the nail on the head when she said that dating guys like George feels like too much pressure. Easier to be the smartest, the wealthiest, and the best-educated member

of the couple. Of course, a whole book could be written on why this logic is hooey, but there you have it. Bottom line: when it comes to school, work, friends, and passions, you've never settled for anything less than stellar. And so it should be with the men you date. Seek out the best, and for goodness' sakes, when the best seek *you* out, say yes.

6. **The Too-Busy Bessie.** A friend who works twelve-hour days at a hectic LA law firm called me recently to complain about her boyfriend of two years—a graduate student who is pursuing his master's degree in fiction writing, and seems to have a lot of free time on his hands, judging from the hours he logs in front of his Xbox each week. He had been spending less and less time with her lately, had no interest in sex, and always complained that her long days at the office and dinners out with friends were to blame for the emotional distance between them. When she told him that he should come along, he balked. "I can't stand your friends," he said. "If I wanted to hang out with a bunch of corporate drones, I'd call my father." Meanwhile, she had recently discovered a $400 charge for a visit to a strip club on his credit card statement—even though she was paying the rent for both of them until he could publish his first novel. After nearly an hour of listening to her talk, I asked if she actually thought this relationship was going to last. "Of course not," she said. "But I'm tired. I can't imagine having to go through a breakup right now, let alone finding someone new to live with. When things die down at work, I'll start giving it some serious

thought." Breaking up with your unworthy boyfriend and finding a man who deserves you isn't an activity that you can program into your Palm Pilot. It's something that you need to do right away, no matter how busy you are, no matter what trip you were planning together for next spring, no matter how comfortable (though annoyed) he makes you feel. While you're wasting your time with him, fantastic guys are passing you by. So dump him now. And if you ask nicely, I'll give you George's number.

7. **The "But He's Changing" Girl.** I remember quite vividly in second grade, when my teacher described how the continents had once been one large landmass but over time they had shifted and separated into seven distinct parts. I was incredibly freaked by this and asked what had happened to all those people who had one foot in, say, Africa, and another in Asia, and no chance to jump onto one piece of land or the other before the split. My teacher laughed kindly and explained that the continental shifts took much longer than the span of one human life—the changes were so slight that no one person could have ever distinguished them. Think of me as your teacher in this moment, laughing (kindly, of course) at you for thinking that your never-got-it-together boyfriend is making steady progress toward being the man you deserve. Like the continents, he might very well be changing, but believe me, that change will be imperceptible to the naked eye and never fast enough to affect your life. My father once gave me a

piece of advice about a slacker ex-boyfriend whom I desperately wanted to turn into a career man, and it was the most useful thing anyone has ever told me. He said, "People can change, but most people don't." If your boyfriend wasn't the man you wanted him to be when you met—emotionally, financially, intellectually, or in any other way—chances are he never will be.

8. **The "But the Sex Is Amazing" Artist.** Oh my dear, are we really having this conversation? It seems to me that a lot of very well educated, ambitious women are only sexually attracted to bad boys and social deviants. Give it a rest. The nice guys of the world can be pretty fantastic between the sheets, too—and they'll actually buy you dinner first (and call the next day).

9. **The "He'll Never Leave Me" Mess.** Being comfortable around your partner is essential. But choosing someone just because he makes you feel safe is never a good idea. Remember the character on *Sex and the City* who whispered to Carrie at her own wedding that you should always find a man who loves you more than you love him? Women the world over were shaking their heads at that line, yet many of us follow this advice in real life. If you find yourself relaxed by the thought that you are better looking than your partner, or smarter, or more ambitious, it's time to call it a day on your lackluster love affair. The ultimate relationship is the one in which you are mutually challenged and impressed by one another. You should never be contented by the idea that you're the best he can get—instead, you should be overjoyed by

the fact that he could have anyone, yet he's chosen you. I briefly dated a well-known New York writer, and I remember worrying that his career was more established than mine. When I told my mother this, she sighed and replied: "You're not dating him. *He's* dating you." Recognize yourself as the prize that you are, and don't settle for anything less than the best.

10. **The "I Just Bought a Book Called *Dating Up*" Woman.** If you're reading this, you've probably already determined that your love life is in dire need of an upgrade. Don't worry. All of us have been there, and there are plenty of concrete things you can do to begin searching for the right guy today. The following pages are packed with tips and advice from women around the country who have survived the trenches of Dateland and ended up with quality men. Yes, hindsight is a bitch. But one of the best ways to learn what to do in relationships is to recognize where we've gone wrong in the past. As a veteran dater in both London and New York—two cities where it's easier to find a cab at four in the morning than it is to find a good man—I've had my share of dating disasters, most of which are documented in the following pages. Despite the disappointment, the false starts, and the evidence to the contrary, there is hope. And there are great men out there—men with good hearts, strong minds, killer bodies, serious bank accounts, and love to spare. Why should you take my word for it? Because I've tried these techniques and shared

them with the frustrated women I know, and they actually work. In other words, I'm not only the Dating Up president. I'm also a client.

## Loserpalooza

So many losers to date, so little time. It is the plight of many a modern woman.

Later on in the book we'll discuss the types of rich men to avoid (because, let's face it, a lot of them suck too). But in general, you should run, not walk, away from a man who exhibits any of the following characteristics, regardless of what's in his wallet:

**He who fears commitment like the plague.** If you were to fall in love with a cactus, that would be most unfortunate. Because no matter how hard you try, no matter how cute you look, a cactus quite simply will not love you back. You might get to admire the cactus from afar, or from right up close if you're lucky, but a cactus cannot be depended upon to call you back, bring you soup when you get sick, or accompany you to your second cousin's wedding in Colorado. Think of any man who will not commit as a cactus. He may be tall and pretty and unusual, but he's not going to budge, and if you get too close to him, it's going to hurt like hell. Whether he has a girlfriend or "just got out of a relationship" or is "afraid of getting hurt" makes no difference. If a man is not interested in a commitment, send him packing. When you meet the right one, he will be so concerned with keeping you all to himself that any fear he has about being tied down will vanish. He will call when he says he's going to, take you out on the weekends (and eventually during the week, too), introduce you to his friends, and refer to you as his girlfriend within three months of your first date.

**He who is a man-child.** You may never get him to stop collecting comic books or slurping up the milk in the bowl after he eats his morning cereal, but a man of a certain age should know how to do certain things. For example: tie a tie, pick up after himself, hold down a job, talk about his feelings, exist in a relationship. Every woman who has ever fallen in love knows that a certain level of training is involved. (My last serious boyfriend was fantastic, but he did not know that sheets needed to be washed. For some unimaginable reason, he thought bedding was a laundry-free zone. Insane, but not a deal breaker. We burned the existing sheets and he started spending a little more quality time with the Tide bottle.) It's important to recognize that you are dating the man, not the man's potential. A couple of weeks ago I was having drinks with a Yale-educated colleague, who told me that her boyfriend of four years was finally thinking about leaving his job with a landscaping company (translation: he mows lawns for a living) and going to community college. "He wants to be an engineer," she said. "And he's just so smart. I feel like he's really starting to get it together." One more glass of Shiraz and I might have screamed "Honey! Wake up. He's thirty-four years old." You know how many term papers and unpaid internships and thankless hours at the office you had to log in before getting any professional credit. Don't think a guy who hasn't gotten his act together so far is going to be able to do so instantaneously just because you want him to.

**He who disrespects women.** Many, many men, regardless of education, income, and breeding, believe that there are two categories of women in the world. The women whom they know, and the Others. The *Others* are those who don't deserve respect or thought. You can identify this sort of man with ease because he'll be the one talking about a woman whom he doesn't know personally as though she were a plastic doll—she might be the waitress with the long legs at his local bar, a stripper in a club, or a porn star on TV. Don't give this sort of man a moment of your time. And for goodness' sakes, *do not* buy into the idea that there are two sorts of women and you just happen to be the lucky sort. Eventually, if a man thinks this way, the two categories are very likely to run together. The men who go to strip clubs or make a lot of sexist jokes are often the same ones who cheat and lie and end up disrespecting you as much as they would a glossy photograph. A man who objectifies women doesn't deserve the company of a strong, smart, successful female. Why do men like this exist? Why do so many people—men *and* women—embrace a "boys will be boys" mentality, even in this day and age, when women have ascended to professional and personal heights? Because there is usually no recourse for the actions of disrespectful men. Why not start a trend? Explain to him that pornography, strippers, and the like are bad for all humankind. If he doesn't agree to get them out of his life, get him out of yours. Which leads us to a particular subset of the same category . . .

**He who hates his mom and/or all of his exes.** I briefly dated a lawyer who seemed rather sweet at first, and on our second date he told me about his ex. "She was hysterical," he said. "Absolutely everything made her crazy. She wanted to talk about our relationship every second, and she didn't trust me at all."

Too bad, I thought. She missed out on a great guy.

A week later we ran into one of his neighbors. She appeared to be nice enough, but when we parted ways he whispered, "That one's hysterical. We made out a few times and then all of a sudden I was supposed to be her boyfriend. Clingy much? Some people are so crazy, you know?"

I nodded. At that point, I started to wonder if he wasn't one of them.

Next it was his mother: "Four missed calls from her! That woman is nuts. She gets hysterical if I don't call her back for a week."

He lasted only a few more days before he became known among my friends as the Walking Hysterical Woman Complex. WHWC for short. I told him I couldn't see him anymore, because I had never heard him say one positive thing about a woman in his life, and I figured it was only a matter of time before I asserted an opinion or made a demand and joined the ranks of the others he'd been with.

"Well that's just insane," he told me.

Exactly.

If a man seems to go on and on about all of his awful exes, don't be flattered that he likes you better. It is fairly unlikely that he has just had a lifelong string of terrible luck, and you are the first and only well-adjusted woman he's ever met. Most likely, six months from now he'll be telling some other poor creature about the time you hysterically asked him to take out the garbage, and how, when he refused, you flew into a rage.

Women with opinions intimidate certain men. Leave these men to someone who doesn't have any.

**He who is an artist of the starving variety.** I've said it before, and I will say it again several times before this book is through: money matters. The starving artist is appealing to so many of us for a couple of reasons. First, his carefree, whimsical lifestyle is refreshing in the face of our own jobs and deadlines and stress. And second, he tends to be ridiculously good looking. When I first moved to New York and worked ten- or twelve-hour days, I dated a gorgeous musician who lived in Brooklyn. I was forever running off to a meeting or an interview. He was forever sitting at home, waiting for inspiration to strike. As I was stressing over my tiny paycheck, he was wondering if he could borrow half of it until his record deal came through.

Our phone calls generally went something like this:

> Me (frantically unwrapping a Lean Cuisine at ten p.m., three minutes after walking in the door from the office): Ugh, my day was awful. How was yours?
>
> Him: Also awful. I got woken up at, like, dawn by my super. He was bitching about the rent being late.
>
> Me: At dawn?
>
> Him: Well, it was noontime. But it felt like dawn.
>
> Me: Uhh-huh.

A man whose career path is so different from your own will probably never understand your stress, your ambition, or your needs. And after a while, his cavernous dimples will seem unimportant compared to his cavernous wallet.

**He whose head on the social totem pole is way the heck lower than yours.** If I had a penny for every time I've heard the question "What on earth does she see in him?" I could have purchased a record label and signed Mr. Dimples myself by now. So many of my female friends are dating down—choosing men who didn't go to college, who lack ambition, or who have no clue about saving for the future. It might sound harsh, but someone who is beneath you in terms of brains, money, or education will not make a good partner. I don't mean that if you didn't both go to Stanford or have matching SAT scores then you're destined for disaster. It's not that cut-and-dried. But equality and understanding are essential in a relationship, and it's hard to achieve either of those things with someone who is quite simply not your equal. Think about your closest friends. I bet that none of them got their GEDs and then started a rock band. Like you, they went to college, they pursued careers, they have it together. Common ground is what good friendships—and romances—are built on.

Now that you know exactly who to avoid (as if you didn't know before), it's time to delete the names of any nonprospects from your phone. And writing them down on a slip of paper that you'll then ask your roommate/best friend/mailman to hide until further notice is a definite nonoption. Because finding a man who deserves you might take a little time. And we don't want to backslide, now, do we? Go on. Delete his name. Don't think about his cute scraggly beard or the way he plays guitar. Think about the last time you went out to dinner and split a six-dollar burrito, which he then asked you to pay for when the check arrived. Think about how his idea of a bed is a futon. How his idea of a job is a paper route. Now delete it.

Good girl. You're ready to start dating up. Here we go.

# Getting Ready

"Genius is of small use to a woman who does not know how to do her hair."

—Edith Wharton

To get a date with the average man, all you need is a mini-skirt, two breasts, and the willpower to ignore his calls for at least a week after giving him your number. But starting a relationship with a quality wealthy man is another matter.

The rich, as they say, are different. To them, summer is a verb, share is a noun, and rent is a passé Broadway musical. Men who are both rich and interesting want to know that the women in their lives can keep up. The good news for you is, you can probably already do that. But there are still adjustments that every one of us can make to look better, become more cultured, and sound informed.

Other dating books tend to advise us in one of two ways when it comes to working on ourselves. These books want us either to change completely and act like little man-pleasing robots (I won't even get into how ridiculous *that* is), or they tell us, "You're the best! If he doesn't want to be with you, he's nuts."

That statement is comforting and all, but it always makes me wonder to whom the writer is talking: *Who* is the best? Me personally? Does the boring girl in my office have a copy that says "You're, umm, boring. If he doesn't want to be with you, I can sort of understand"? We can't all be the best in every way. But if we want the greatest guys the world has to offer, we need to bring something to the table. The first part of finding Mr. Right is being ready when he appears, and a man of quality needs a woman who can keep up—someone who will look the part and act the part, too. This chapter offers an overview of the most essential topics that appeal to someone who is both cultured (such as art and wine) and male (such as sports and dude movies). These are all areas that you should (and possibly do) know a bit about anyway. But there is always more to learn. The best sort of man is informed, inquisitive, and interested in knowing about a wide range of topics. And the best sort of woman is no different.

## Drugstore Cowgirls

As your mother probably told you when you were going through that gawky adolescent stage, it's what's inside that counts. But it's what's outside that your future husband will notice first. So let's begin there.

When I worked in the Condé Nast building in Times Square—an office space that has more beautiful women per square inch than some Midwestern states have, period—my stock among my male friends immediately went up. I suddenly knew women who worked at *Allure, Vogue, Glamour, Self, Lucky*—and every guy I knew wanted to be set up.

I love matchmaking, so this was no problem. The first pair I introduced was Jack and Ellen. Jack works as a banker on Wall Street, Ellen as a beauty editor. They decided to meet for dinner at Balthazar on a Thursday night. That afternoon, I e-mailed Jack to see how he was planning to prepare.

*I'm going straight from work,* he wrote back. *Why? Am I supposed to change or something?*

Meanwhile, Ellen searched in the fashion closet for some fabulous new thing to wear. When you work at a women's magazine, you have access to all the designer clothes you could ever want, and if you spilled the contents of your desk drawers onto the floor, an entire Sephora franchise might very well fall out. So Ellen didn't need to go home before the date, either. Instead, she applied her concealer, foundation, bronzer, eyeliner, mascara, and lip gloss right in her office. When she was done, she looked like Ellen—beautiful and perfectly put-together.

Jack called me after the date, and the first thing he said was, "She's gorgeous. I love how she doesn't wear any makeup. Women look so much better when they go the natural route."

I was floored. But it happened again and again. I'd set up my wealthy male friends with editors, and the guys would always comment on how little makeup the women wore. Because, of course, like all men, they think they love low-maintenance girls.

Bless their ignorant hearts.

What these men don't know (and let's keep it that way) is that it took years of experimenting with different makeup shades and textures to make those beauty editors look so darn natural. Flawless makeup applications leave you looking like you're not wearing any makeup at all. And, as I learned from working in magazines, you don't always have to go with the most expensive products to achieve the perfect look.

In Manhattan, uptown girls often stroll down the makeup aisle of Duane Reade Drug. Why? Because women who can actually afford high-end cosmetics know that some things are worth the money, while others are interchangeable with their cheaper counterparts. Learn to know the difference, and don't be swayed by fancy packaging.

Always read the ingredient list. For example, the main ingredients in a bottle of CVS-brand Balanced Care Conditioner (retail value: $3.00) are water, cetearyl alcohol, cetyl alcohol, and stearyl alcohol. The main ingredients in a bottle of Kerastase Oleo-Relax (retail value: $16.00) are water, cetearyl alcohol, glycerin, and cetyl esters.

Yup, that's right. Pretty much the exact same ingredients. And do you know what all those alcohols and esters do to your hair?

Neither do I. I'm guessing they make it clean.

Cosmetics, shampoos, conditioners, exfoliators, and body creams are physical enhancers. You don't need a license to operate them, and they don't come with an owner's manual, so it's fine to go with the cheaper option when it's presented to you.

## Top Ten Products for Under Ten Bucks

These tried-and-true cheapies are just as good (and in some cases, even better) than their department store doppelgangers.

1. **Maybelline New York Great Lash Mascara ($5.29).** A best-kept secret of beauty editors, this is the most long-lasting and impressive mascara out there, period. Buy it in Blackest Black for lashes that just won't quit.
2. **Cover Girl Trublend Makeup Foundation ($5.79).** The foundation you wore in high school is still one of the finest. And, as in high school, it won't cost you your entire allowance. Feel free to buy the newest issue of *Tiger Beat* with the leftover cash.
3. **Cover Girl Invisible Concealer ($5.79).** A few dabs of this stuff, and blemishes and under-eye circles vanish. When people tell you that you look refreshed and ask where you've been, say Waikiki, not Walgreens.
4. **Maybelline Expert Eyes Twin Brow and Eye Pencil ($2.99).** Products that multitask are the answer to a working girl's prayers. Products that multitask, make you look fabulous, and cost under three bucks are worthy of worship. Bow down.
5. **Cetaphil Gentle Skin Cleanser ($7.39).** Backstage at fashion shows, this stuff is flowing like Evian. It cleanses skin gently and thoroughly, and can be applied to a wet or dry face.

6. **Lush Buffy the Backside Slayer Body Butter ($8.15).** A friend in London introduced me to this skin-sloughing miracle. Seriously, it's worth crossing the Atlantic for. But luckily you won't have to, because Lush stores are popping up in cities all over the United States, and you can buy online at www.lush.com.

7. **Eucerin Dry Skin Therapy Calming Cream ($7.99).** Sort of like the little black dress of moisturizers, this unscented cream is subtle and soft, and it will make men want to touch your legs. Need I say more?

8. **Neutrogena Triple Moisture Daily Deep Conditioner ($6.00).** This lives beside Kerastase and Garren on my shower's conditioner shelf (another bonus of working in magazines is that you never have to buy your own beauty products again. Otherwise, I'd probably be riding the Suave train), and of them all it's my absolute favorite. Leave it on for three minutes and rinse. Hair is TV-commercial shiny and soft. Go ahead, give it a swing.

9. **Clean and Clear Absorbing Sheets ($5.49 for 50).** Some companies charge such a fortune for papers that get rid of those gross little oily spots, you'd think you were going to frame them afterward. These sheets leave skin matte for hours, but aren't overly powdery (or expensive).

10. **Smith's Rosebud Salve ($5.00).** Romance can be tempestuous, but lip balm—like shoes and bags—loves you unconditionally. This one leaves your lips soft, shiny, and lightly scented (also comes in strawberry), and you can use it on dry hands, too.

## Foolproof Tips for Applying Your Makeup Before a Big Date

1. Always begin by washing your face with a mild exfoliator like St. Ives Apricot Scrub, and follow with a lightweight moisturizer.
2. If your skin is relatively clear, use a tinted moisturizer to even out the tone instead of foundation—it provides lighter coverage for a more natural look. If you have blemishes in certain areas but not others, try dabbing a maximum-coverage foundation on them as concealer, then combine a bit of the same foundation with a lightweight moisturizer and apply the mixture all over. This works better (and is a lot cheaper) than using a separate concealer and foundation, because the colors are a perfect match.
3. Curl your eyelashes twice (for thirty seconds each time) with a heated eyelash curler (put it under your blow dryer for a few seconds but make sure not to burn yourself. Ouch!) before applying mascara. Some of the best mascaras are the ones from companies like Boujoirs, with white mascara on one end and black on the other. Apply the white first as a primer, then do two coats of black. This will make lashes appear fuller and hold the color longer.
4. Straight-up pink blushes are on the decline, as are orangey bronzers that leave you looking like an

Oompa-Loompa. The best bet for any skin tone is a product that combines bronzing powder and a hint of pink, such as Cargo's Miami Beach, or the famous Orgasm blush from Nars. Gel bronzers like Clinique's True Bronze bronzing gel give skin a nice, translucent effect, but you have to be fast if you don't want to look like a streaky mess, since they dry in about ten seconds. If you want to apply bronzer all over, not just on your face, bear this in mind: a makeup artist at a cover shoot once told me that Make Up For Ever bronzer was used on the set of *Baywatch*, because it's waterproof, lasts all day, and doesn't rub off on fabric.

5. Before applying lipstick, cover your lips with a thin layer of foundation and let it dry for thirty seconds—that way you get the exact shade that you see in the tube, rather than a mixture of the shade and your own lip color. The foundation also helps to set your lipstick, so it lasts hours longer than it otherwise would.

While the drugstore is fabulous for buying colors to experiment with, you should splurge on a few makeup essentials. I use Chanel's tinted moisturizer—it smells faintly of roses—which gets tucked into my purse next to Neutrogena pressed powder and Chap Stick. It's nice to have one or two special products. They give you a little confidence boost. But repeat after me: when purchasing expensive, department-store beauty products, always try before you buy. It's important to see what your makeup will look like in outdoor light, how it settles after a couple of hours, and how your skin reacts to it the next day. Resist the temptation to buy cosmetics right after you put them on—they're not going anywhere and even the pushiest salesperson won't hold it against you if you use the old "I'm going to have to think about it" line. (Just be sure to get her name so that she'll receive the commission when you come back.) Once you know what you like, you won't have to do the repeat performance thing again. Plus, going back to the counter means you'll get to snag twice as many free samples (companies like Kiehl's and Prescriptives are especially great for this).

The try-before-you-buy mentality is doubly important when deciding on a perfume. A scent needs at least an hour to settle into your skin and mix with your natural oils before you can tell how it will smell for the rest of the day. At the perfume counter, tell the salesperson what you like in general terms (spicy, floral, fruity, etc.) and dab different formulas inside your elbows, on your wrists, behind your knees, and on your neck (don't rub it in because that crushes the molecules and breaks down the scent). Again, ask for samples.

## Leave It to the Pros

There are some beauty decisions that every girl must make for herself. One of these is determining which treatments she can do at home and which ones she'll need to consult a professional on (and dole out her hard-earned cash for). A good rule of thumb is that waxing and hair cutting are best left to the pros (remembering how my bangs looked when my mom cut them in fourth grade always makes me more than happy to hand over my Visa card to the receptionist at Vidal Sassoon).

## Parting Is Such Sweet Sorrow: When to Say Sayonara to Your Makeup

All good things must come to an end, and that's especially true of your makeup. There's a difference between thrifty and unsanitary. Here's how to know when to call it a day.

**Mascara.** Because the brush comes into direct contact with your eyes on a daily basis, it will start to grow bacteria after just three months.

**Foundation.** Chuck it if its contents still don't blend after a few shakes of the bottle. Once the oils have separated, it won't go on as smoothly.

**Eye pencils.** It's time to get rid of these when they get a white film that doesn't go away with sharpening.

**Lipstick.** Probably fine for up to six months. However, show me the woman who's actually kept a lipstick that long and I'll show you a woman who needs to be wearing more lipstick. You can usually tell that a lipstick has passed its prime when it starts to dry out and won't spread easily.

**Sponges/Brushes.** Toss a sponge after just five or six uses. Brushes can stay around for up to two years, as long as you wash them regularly with soap and warm water.

Many women I know spend tons of money on manicures and pedicures every month, and wouldn't have it any other way. Personally, I think it's just as effective and relaxing to flop down on the couch with a glass of Pinot Grigio and a bottle of OPI's Pinking of You. But that's just me.

Hair color is also up to you. I probably wouldn't attempt it myself at home (not since the Manic Panic massacre of 1993), but I know lots of beauty editors who do. Some at-home brands aren't too bad—Goldwell and L'Oreal actually include moisturizing ingredients and add tons of shine to your hair.

When you do decide to go pro, there are plenty of ways to do it on the cheap. Places that are just opening will have good deals, so keep an eye out. Most salons provide discounts if you refer a friend or are a new customer. Many hair salons and spas (including Aveda, Bumble and Bumble, Frederic Fekkai, and Vidal Sassoon) have training schools for student stylists, where you can get a cut, color, or waxing at a reduced rate. You'll have to wait a little longer, though (and, in the case of hair, each salon has its own rules—some require you to get a drastic cut, others make you sit and wait for hours while teachers survey their students' work). At salons and spas without training facilities, always get the name of the best person on staff and ask if her assistants do treatments. Having been trained by the best, and still eager to please, they'll do the same work for next to nothing.

## Clothes Encounters

Speaking of getting something for next to nothing, I want to let you in on a little secret. The majority of twenty-something magazine editors in Manhattan (including me, back in the day) make about as much money now as they did from their afternoon babysitting jobs in high school. Yet these women dress like they've just walked off a runway. How do they afford it? You might say necessity is the mother of invention, if by necessity you mean Prada bags and Chanel sweater sets. It's easy to live a life of high fashion on a budget—the sort of life that attracts interesting rich men (and makes the aforementioned budget a thing of the past).

Most men can't tell the difference between a black pencil skirt from Gucci and a black pencil skirt from the Gap. Those who can are probably a little too high-maintenance (read: gay) for your purposes anyway. As with beauty products, do not be afraid to mix high- and low-end clothes. It's worth making an investment in a few quality staple pieces, then supplementing with fun things from H&M.

The ten essential pieces that no girl should be without are as follows. Be willing to get them through whatever means necessary (gaining credit card debt, working a second job, signing over your firstborn child, etc.). These are the items that will see you through any date—be it dinner and dancing, or bowling and beers:

1. **A little black dress.** For two years I had a black halter dress from Banana Republic that never failed to lure the boys. That thing was like catnip for the Ivy League set, and it cost me only fifty bucks. Note: no matter how great you look in it, and no matter which man will be there, you can't wear your LBD to an afternoon barbeque, dentist appointment, child's birthday party, or

car wash (or so my friends tell me . . .). As with tequila, admit that it's good, but know your limit.

2. **A pretty cotton dress or skirt.** If you can't wear your LBD for a trip to the park, what *can* you wear? This is your answer. You'll look pretty, but not too formal; sexy, but not too provocative. Avoid a top that goes straight across if you're busty—instead, aim for a halter or scoop neck. And no matter what your legs look like, make sure the dress covers your knees. Pair it with strappy sandals (don't even think of wearing flip-flops).

3. **The perfect jeans.** The dressing room lines in the denim departments at Barneys and Bloomingdale's are a testament to the popularity of designer labels, but I think the Gap still gives them a run for their money if you're willing to sort through some not-so-flattering styles (read: straight-legged) to get to the good stuff. Aim for a pair that is low-waisted and slightly flared at the bottom. Darker versions are more forgiving and flattering for curvy figures, but may fade quickly. To reduce fading, always wash your jeans inside out in cold water. And throw them in the dryer for the ultimate stomach suction.

4. **Black pants.** I personally can't get enough of the Editor pants at Express—you want black pants that are a bit stretchy and flared but not too tight; better to go up a size than to show your panty line to the world. Pair with sandals or sexy pumps.

5. **One pair of three-inch black pumps.** These babies can take you anywhere (even if you do have to take a cab

three blocks to get there in them). Perfect for work, parties, or shopping (if your feet can handle it), or basically any day when you want to make your legs look longer and thinner. Just be sure to avoid subway grates and replace the soles once they start to get worn—usually every three months or so if you wear them often.

6. **One pair of stylish sneakers.** Please don't ever be that girl who wears stilettos to a Yankees game. In your arsenal of date clothes, you should have at least one pair of stylish sneakers (they exist, I swear). Think Puma rather than Nike.

7. **A trench coat.** If you've ever watched Audrey Hepburn run through the rain in the final scene of *Breakfast at Tiffany's,* I don't need to tell you why this one's a must. A classic coat in black or camel is best.

8. **Jackie O sunglasses.** Slide a pair on all year round to add an effortless hint of style and sophistication to any outfit. But don't wear them indoors unless you are:

   a. Anna Wintour

   b. Extremely hungover

   c. Recently back from a boxing ring.

9. **A great bathing suit.** You never know when a new man will fly you off to Bermuda, and frankly my dear, your Speedo isn't going to cut it on a romantic weekend getaway. If you have a slammin' body, by all means, wear a string bikini. For the other 99 percent of us, bear these tips in mind: for a boyish figure, go for bold patterns

that will accentuate your slight curves, and try a two-piece with shorts on the bottom instead of a skimpy traditional cut; if you have big breasts, diagonal stripes can make them appear smaller, and a band right underneath can give the illusion of lift; if your hips are wide, try a two-piece with a skirted bottom.

10. **Sexy lingerie.** A good rule of thumb for the first several dates with a new guy is to wear your rattiest, holiest granny panties under your adorable outfit. This way, if you're tempted to go home with him before it's a good idea, you will hopefully be too mortified by the prospect of him seeing your underwear to actually go through with it. But once you are ready, hit Victoria's Secret and try to look away from the cash register when they ring you up. Aim for sexy but sophisticated styles that make you feel hot (this is the most important part). If you're comfortable in a lace thong, go for it, but if girly satin panties are more your speed, don't worry—your man will be happy either way.

## Cut-Rate Couture

There are two ways to find discounted couture clothing.

The first is sample sales: go early, since most of the good stuff gets snapped up fast, and don't expect a dressing room. You'll most likely have to change in front of everyone, so if you're feeling modest, wear a bathing suit or tight yoga pants under your clothes. A list of upcoming sample sales in your city can be found at www.dailycandy.com.

The second way to get a closet full of couture is thrift store shopping. Pound the pavement, or try these Web sites:

www.thesnob.com

www.ritzconsignment.com

www.jillsconsignment.com

www.turnaboutshoppe.com

www.findoutlet.com

With both makeup and clothes, once you have a sense of what you like, you can buy duplicates at a reduced price online. For discounted duds, try:

www.overstock.com

www.amerimark.com

## Time Is Money

Now that we've ensured that you'll look great, it's time to think about what you'll say and do when your future husband approaches. Generally speaking, "I've just bought a whole bunch of makeup and clothes in the hopes of meeting a great guy, and doggone, it worked!" does not make a very successful opening line. To find the sort of man you want, you have to broaden your horizons, and familiarize yourself with a range of topics, including travel, art, film, literature, politics, food, and wine. From the very first time you speak to him, you'll want to make it clear that you are confident, intelligent, and worldly enough to hold your own with any crowd. Knowledge of these things will help you do just that. And they might help you land a great job or business deal in addition to a new boyfriend.

## Travel on the Cheap

The most interesting men are almost always well traveled, and they will expect their future wives to be, too (sorry, but your eighth-grade class trip to Niagara Falls doesn't count). The good news is that these days virtually everyone has studied abroad for at least a semester, so you probably have some experience under your belt. The bad news is that these days virtually everyone has studied abroad for at least a semester, so you probably won't dazzle him with your tales of swigging Bud Light at the Texas Embassy in London for three months with a bunch of kids from the University of Michigan.

Fear not. It's possible to see the world on a budget. Travel is truly one of the best investments you can make. Just think: skip one dinner out, one trip to Zara, and two nights at the bar, and you can probably buy yourself a ticket to Greece. I traveled all around Europe for a year, and now that I live in New York I find that that experience gives me something to talk about with anyone—be it the time I went to Mardi Gras in a small village in Belgium, the month I spent hiking in the wine country in France, or the night I put my embarrassing childhood Irish step dancing classes to good use in a Galway pub, my travels have provided me with stories to tell for a lifetime.

One last added bonus of travel: it teaches you to exist outside of your comfort zone, which will probably come in handy when your wealthy boyfriend takes you home to meet his parents in their twenty-four-room mansion.

**Getting there.** Most airlines send out a weekly e-mail to customers highlighting the best new discounts available (register on their Web sites). American Airlines has a particularly good plan called Net SAAvers (www.aa.com), which lets you search for discounted flights to destinations all over the world. If you don't feel like having your inbox full of reduced-rate flight alerts, log on to www.travelzoo.com and register for the weekly Top 20 e-mail—it's basically a roundup of the cheapest flights being offered on any airline.

My super-thrifty friend Aliya taught me this trick—go to www.expedia.com to find the most affordable flight to your chosen destination, and then buy it directly through the airline. That way you avoid paying extra fees and you can change your flight without being hit by huge cancellation charges. Once you arrive overseas, it's even cheaper to fly from place to place. Two discount airlines—Ryanair and easyJet—offer unbelievable rates within Europe. I once flew from London to Brussels for a pound on Ryanair! If you're traveling within Europe, it's also a good idea to invest in a Eurail pass (www.eurail.com). This will let you do an unlimited amount of traveling between countries for only a few hundred dollars.

**Choosing hotels.** Book hotel rooms as far ahead of time as possible, and keep your eye out for any special offers. A one- or two-star hotel in the center of the city is fine if you can't afford something nicer—you probably won't be spending much time there anyway. Just make sure that it's clean and safe.

**Dining out.** When traveling abroad, you'll obviously want to sample the local food. But in order to stretch your money, try to eat only one major meal a day. When I was traveling with friends in Italy and France, we'd grab bread and cheese at a local market for lunch and then have extravagant dinners in lovely little cafés. When you're busy sightseeing, who wants to stop that often to eat anyway? Do your wallet and your waistline a favor and keep meals in restaurants to a minimum.

**Shopping.** Resist the urge to buy the first fabulous jacket you see at a thrift store in Barcelona, or the first fifty-Euro box of chocolates you lay eyes on in Brussels. Instead, wait until the last day of your trip—if you still want that coveted possession after seeing what else is out there, then by all means buy it. But remember: shopping is like dating. Don't be tempted to settle for the first seemingly great thing you see. There may be something even better right around the corner.

**Sightseeing.** In every major city in the world, it's possible to spend a small fortune on sightseeing alone. But tourist attractions that cost a lot of money tend to be the most gimmicky and the least interesting. If you want to get to know a place and have an adventure there, walk, visit museums, do free things, hang out where the locals go, and ask a cab driver to show you points of interest instead of climbing on board a bright red tour bus.

**Changing money.** Change money at your local bank ahead of time to save on service fees. If you need to change more money once you arrive overseas, it's best to do it at an ATM, and take out all you'll need at once rather than going back again and again, since both the foreign bank and your bank at home will charge you a small fee for processing.

**Speaking the language.** Americans have an embarrassing tendency to think that speaking English loudly is the equivalent of learning a foreign language. When traveling abroad, familiarize yourself with basic phrases such as *yes, no, please, thank you, Can you tell me how to get to? How much does it cost?* and (if you must) *Do you speak English?*

**Staying safe.** It's a big, exciting world out there. And it's also a little bit scary sometimes. When traveling alone or with female friends, familiarize yourself with your surroundings. Make sure you know how to get in touch with the police and the nearest American embassy. Don't travel with valuables, and store your passport and credit cards in a hotel safe. It's also a good idea to keep a photocopy of your passport with you (and leave another copy at home with someone trustworthy). That way, if yours gets lost or stolen, you can easily prove who you are to the State Department and expedite the issuing of a new one.

**Splurging.** Why is it important to save your pennies while traveling? So you can treat yourself to something luxurious at the end of your trip, of course! Stay one night in a great hotel or eat at least one meal somewhere insanely expensive and drink at the bar afterward—you could meet a very rich man, so think of it as an investment in the future (one that's a hell of a lot more fun than your Roth IRA). During college, my friend Sandra went to the south of France alone for three weeks and stayed in youth hostels. But the night before she was due to fly back home to Boston, she checked into a fabulous spa and resort. It was there, in the massage prep room, that she met a businessman with a house in Bordeaux. Needless to say, Sandra missed her flight home. She stayed in France for another month and she didn't swipe her credit card once.

## Wine

An all-expenses-paid trip to the south of France is a great way to learn about many topics: good food, romance, Edith Piaf, and above all, wine. Alas, not all of us are so lucky.

Let's play a word association game. If I say "salt," you think *shaker.* If I say "shopping," you think *bag.* If I say "wine," you think . . . if the word *cooler* popped into your head, you've got a lot of work to do.

Cultured men are impressed by a woman who knows how to order wine. When he asks you what you'd like to drink at dinner, an answer like "Oh whatever—something white" is fine, but it's not exactly going to knock his socks off. Remember that from the moment you meet him, your man is sizing you up to see if you're marriage material—the same thing you're doing to him. Not that anyone ever got the three-carat Harry Winston just because she knew her Bordeaux from her Burgundy, but every little bit helps.

The first thing to do is find a wine shop in your area. Get to know the people who work there, and ask them for advice and lots of samples (hey, it's for research). Many shops have weekly tastings, where you can try new wines and learn about their origins. Some even offer classes, which can be informative, since the best way to understand wine is simply to drink it. Not to mention, the caliber of man who attends these events is pretty darn high. Once you know what you like, you can often get it at a reduced price if you buy by the case. And some places will sell you mixed cases if you ask nicely.

Perhaps you prefer to learn about wine by drinking copious amounts of it at home. May I suggest www.wine.com. This Web site is a valuable tool for learning about and buying wine, with detailed descriptions of wines from around the world, information on joining wine clubs, and the best sales and specials I've ever seen. Also, their staff is incredible. E-mail them any question, and they'll get back to you right away.

If you already know a thing or two about wine and want to learn more, the University of California at Davis offers a distance course. Check out their Web site at www.wineserver.ucdavis.edu. But if you're not planning to become a sommelier anytime soon and just want a cheat sheet, here are the most common wines, broken up into bubblies, reds, and whites.

## Bubbly

Hopefully your union with a smart, financially secure man will lead to fewer nights sipping seltzer on the couch, and more nights on the town drinking a far superior bubbly beverage: Champagne. The only true Champagnes are those made in the Champagne region of Northern France from a blend of Chardonnay, Pinot Noir, and Pinot Meunier grapes. Champagnes labeled Brut Absolut, Brut, and Extra-Dry will have a dry, refreshing taste, while those labeled Sec, Demi-Sec, and Doux are sweeter. Champagne is not like beauty products—here, the price tag matters. The more expensive, the better it will taste, and cheap Champagnes are pretty ghastly.

For bubbly on a budget, try a sparkling wine instead

(these are basically the same, but cannot be called Champagne because they weren't grown in that region). The best of them use the same laborious method that is used to create Champagne. One particularly good (and cheap) sparkling wine is Cava, a fruity, delicious version grown in Spain.

**Serving bubbly.** When serving bubbly at home, make sure that it is well chilled (it should sit in the fridge overnight, if possible). Unlike other wines, once you open it, bubbly can't be recorked, so you won't be able to put it back in the fridge between rounds. Keep an ice bucket on hand, and store your bubbly there to keep it cool all night (or for the half hour it takes you to down the bottle).

## Red Wines

- **Cabernet Sauvignon.** The primary flavors of Cabernet are heavy, dark fruits like black currant and blackberry. Interesting versions, like interesting men, hail from all over the world—Italy, Spain, Australia, Chile, Argentina, and California. The best Cabernets are medium- to full-bodied and very dark in color. Often blended with other wines to detract from its heaviness, straight-up Cabernet isn't meant for sipping on its own—definitely serve with a hearty food that can keep up.
- **Chianti.** Chianti hails from the region of the same name in Tuscany. (If you like the wine, why not invest in a country home? It will save on shipping.) It is made from a blend of grapes: the most pronounced is

Sangiovese, but it may also contain Cabernet Sauvignon and others. The best Chiantis have a slight floral taste, and should be served with (what else?) pastas and Italian dishes with red sauce, such as chicken Parmesan.

- **Merlot.** Merlots are generally full-bodied and dark in color, but they are less heavy than Cabernets. Because of this, they can be sipped on their own and still hold up when served with food (best with warm, home-cooked suburban sort of meals like roast beef or chicken—also great with takeout pizza). Merlot is full of fruity flavors—particularly cherry and plum. It gets blended with Cabernet Sauvignon to make almost all Bordeaux reds. Some cheap wines can be delicious, but Merlot ain't one of them. If you're in the mood for it, splurge. Some of the best Merlots are made in California. Other good versions come from Oregon, France, Italy, and New Zealand.

- **Pinot Noir.** You may remember me from *Sideways.* Pinot Noir is like the ultimate dating fantasy (the one we're not indulging anymore). Winemakers who produce it like a challenge. They take the most difficult, fickle grapes, and painstakingly tend to them in the hopes that the perfect wine will be the outcome (tell me you never tried this on one of your difficult, fickle exes). In some cases (particularly in Oregon, California, and France), it actually works, and the resulting wine is absolute heaven—soft, perfumed, fruity deliciousness (older Pinots tend to be more earthy). But Pinot Noir is one of the easiest wines to mess up, and rather yucky versions exist everywhere. As with Merlot, you'll have to shell out some cash to get the best. Serve with fish or dark, rich poultry, like duck.

- **Syrah/Shiraz.** Syrah is a spicy, show-stopping wine that has long been a central player in the Rhône region of France. More recently, it's become enormously popular in Australia (where it is called Shiraz, and often blended with Cabernet Sauvignon). Some of the best comes out of Australia, and it's easy to find a really good bottle for next to nothing. I always have a steady supply of Yellow Tail Shiraz (about seven dollars a bottle) on hand. It's best with spicy stews or just on its own. Syrah is made in various styles and can range from soft- and medium-bodied with berry flavors to deeply colored, bold, and peppery. It has a distinct chocolate-y undertone that makes it the perfect after-dinner wine.

**Serving reds.** Most people think that red wine should be drunk at room temperature. In fact, the best temperature at which to enjoy its various flavors is at about sixty-five degrees Fahrenheit. Store red wine in a cool, dark place until ten minutes before serving. Then pop the whole bottle in the fridge to slightly lower its temperature. The resulting flavor will be more robust and full.

### White Wines

- **Chardonnay.** Chardonnay is well known among wine connoisseurs for being the grape used to make France's beloved white Burgundies and Champagne. But here's what the average wine drinker needs to know: Chardonnay is the Cabernet of whites. The most-often drunk white wine, Chardonnay can be rich and delicious, with hints of apple, honey, fig, and nuts. Some versions tend to be overly oak-y, because Chardonnay is stored in oak barrels (which help bring out its flavor if used correctly). Look for a label that says the wine is lightly oaked or unoaked, from California, Australia, or the south of France. Serve Chardonnay with creamy pastas or fish. Like Cabernet, it's not very good on its own.

- **Pinot Gris/Grigio.** If ever you go for drinks with a bunch of female magazine editors, and you are the first to order, ask for a glass of Pinot. I guarantee the entire table will follow your lead. Pinot Gris is a dark white wine that tends to be dry, crisp, and subtle—not unlike the Chanel suits worn by all those magazine editors. It's originally from northeast Italy (where it is called Pinot Grigio), but has more recently been produced with lots of success in Oregon. Since it isn't aged in oak, Pinot doesn't have that wood-y taste that Chardonnay often gets. Instead, it has hints of peaches and nuts. Serve with a light food like grilled chicken or Caesar salad.

- **Riesling.** Rieslings are very light and fruity, often tasting of apples, and sometimes extremely sweet. The best ones hail from Germany and Alsace, and make a great accompaniment to dessert, or to a light dish like white fish or sushi.

- **Sauvignon Blanc.** One of the lightest and most affordable whites out there, Sauvignon Blanc can taste grassy (Bordeaux versions) or fruity, with hints of melon, berries, and asparagus (New Zealand). It ages well (you can keep it around forever—though if you're anything like me, wine and cookies never make it anywhere near their expiration dates in your kitchen) and can be served on its own or with vegetable-based starters, like a tomato and mozzarella platter.

**Serving whites.** Like ice cream cake or revenge, white wines are best served cold—but not too cold. Refrigerate until twenty minutes before you plan to serve, and then remove the bottle from the fridge to allow a bit of the chill to drop off. This helps flavors peak and makes for a refreshing glass of wine.

## Pairing Wine with Food

There are no hard and fast rules for pairing food and wine. In general, the color principle holds true (white with light foods, red with dark), but only because the lighter the food (in terms of richness, not color) the more it brings out the complementary flavors in a light wine. That said, as in love, opposites attract—a soft red can hold up against a hearty fish like salmon, and a full-bodied white can nicely balance out a heavy roast. Feel free to experiment with different varieties. White wine usually goes best with chicken, fish, entrée salads, creamy pastas, Indian curries, sushi, and Japanese or Thai cuisine. Red tends to go best with red meat, heavy stews, pastas with tomato sauce, and cheese.

## A Recipe for Love

Knowing how to pair food and wine is a good skill to have while dining out, but it's even more imperative when you're eating at home. And guess what?—the next step in getting prepared to meet the man of your dreams is hitting the kitchen.

While I was doing research for this book, a close group of five female friends whom I know socially all got engaged to wealthy businessmen within a month of each other. Of course I had to ask them their secret. All of them are independent career women with varied interests and a lot to offer. But after a decade of fruitless dating in Manhattan, they had decided to take a traditional approach to courtship. No more paying on dates, no more refusing to let men hail them cabs or walk them home. They were going to find gentlemen in New York if it killed them. The funny thing was, as soon as they made this decision, all of them found guys who were more than willing to oblige.

A lot of men want to be gentlemanly, but they are petrified of making us feel disempowered. As one guy I interviewed put it, "I'm more than happy to pay on dates. But some girls are offended if you pay the check. Others just expect that you will. How am I supposed to tell the difference?"

Well, in the case of these five women, the difference was clear. They never opened their wallets, or even a door, while out on a date with their would-be husbands.

But, I asked them, didn't they feel guilty? After years of going dutch and showing men that they were self-sufficient, didn't it feel awkward to suddenly act like the little woman all the time?

No, they said. Because there was still equality, just not of the "you pay the check tonight, and I'll get it next time" variety. Instead, the men always paid, and the women brought something else to the equation: domestic perfection. They'd invite their men over for home-cooked meals and take care of every detail. The table was set, the food perfectly timed, the wine chilled, the candles lit.

"When he walked in the door, I wanted him to feel instantly relaxed," one of them told me. "And on those nights, he never had to do a thing. I wouldn't let him wash so much as a dish, and I didn't ever act flustered. Everything was taken care of—the food, the wine, the dessert. It's not enough to serve filet mignon with a package of Twinkies afterward. It has to be a perfectly orchestrated event. And your apartment shouldn't be a mess. No dishes in the sink, even if you have to wash them as you go while you're cooking. Whenever my boyfriend came to dinner, it looked like I did that sort of thing every night. Which is a huge lie, of course. But he didn't have to know that yet."

All of these women have hectic careers, and refrigerators that contain more film and Veuve Clicquot than actual food. According to them, however, creating a night of domestic perfection is easy if you use the same skill set that you activate to get the job done at work: multitasking, emphasis on timing, and practice. Each of them worked hard to master three or four recipes, complete with side dishes and desserts. They then chose the perfect musical accompaniments, lighting, and table settings.

If this is making you want to retch, I understand. I'm certainly not advocating that you try to convince your new man that you're something you're not. And you clearly don't have the time or inclination to be standing in the kitchen in an apron, ready to hand him his martini when he returns home from a busy day at the office. But what's the harm in playing the perfect housewife every now and then? Yeah, it's a throwback. But it works. And it will help to assuage some of your guilt when you let him pay the check each and every time you go out together.

Here are three easy sample dinners (all of them my mom's creations, and all of them fantastic). Your man will appreciate the effort, even if he knows that you're only pretending to be a happy homemaker. If you haven't met him yet, practice on your friends. The best way to master the timing of a meal is to make it again and again, so by the time he shows up, you'll be an old pro.

## Italian Night

This is one of my mom's most show-stopping dinners. An ex called me three weeks after I broke up with him to say, "I'm doing okay. But I miss your chicken, broccoli, and ziti." It's an over-the-top, calorie-laden meal that's perfect for cold winter nights, and it's delicious. But beware: do not serve to one of those body-conscious guys who weighs himself every morning unless you want to have him crying on your shoulder twelve hours after dinner is served.

### Chicken Broccoli and Ziti

1 head broccoli
3 tablespoons of olive oil,
    plus 1 teaspoon for the boiling water
Dash of salt
2 or 3 boneless chicken breasts
½ cup (one stick) butter
5 ounces shredded Pecorino Romano cheese
5 ounces shredded Parmesan cheese
1 pint light cream
1 pound ziti

Chop broccoli. Set aside.

Place a large saucepan of water on high heat to boil (add the teaspoon of olive oil and a few dashes of salt).

Sautée the chicken breasts in the olive oil in a frying pan. Once it's cooked, remove chicken from the pan. Set aside.

Melt the butter in a saucepan on very low heat, and gradually add the Romano cheese, the Parmesan cheese, and the light cream. Stir frequently and keep the heat as low as possible to avoid burning the sauce.

Once the water is boiling, drop the broccoli in and remove it as soon as it slides off a fork when speared (usually just a couple of minutes or so later). Add ziti to the same pot of boiling water, and cook as directed.

While the pasta cooks, cut the chicken into 1-inch chunks. Drain pasta, and place in a large serving bowl. Add chicken and broccoli, and pour the cream sauce over the top. Use serving spoons to toss.

*Serve with:* Garlic bread and a garden salad. For dessert, a fruit-based tart (you don't have to make it from scratch, but hide the bakery box if you buy it) or vanilla gelato with mixed berries on top.

*The wine:* A light and fruity white will offset the heaviness of this dish. Try a Riesling, Pinot Grigio, or Chardonnay.

*The music:* An album that's romantic, traditional, and mellow, like Dean Martin's *Italian Love Songs,* or Frank Sinatra's *A Fine Romance.*

## Mexican Night

When my mom makes enchiladas or burritos, the food tastes so good and so authentic that we almost forget we are the whitest family on earth. This spicy, yummy meal works best on a Friday night in summertime. Serve on your front porch, if you have one (or, in the case of New Yorkers, on your fire escape).

### Burritos with Chicken or Beef

Olive oil
2 onions
2 red peppers
2 green peppers
Boneless chicken breast or ground hamburger meat
Old El Paso seasoning mix
12-inch tortillas
1 can refried beans
2 tomatoes
8 ounces Monterey Jack cheese, shredded

Pour some olive oil into a frying pan, and heat it for a minute or two on medium heat. Add the onions and peppers (chopped), and once they're browned, throw in the meat and cook on medium-high heat until no longer pink.

If you're kitchen-savvy, there are many homemade spice combinations you can whip up, but if not, Old El Paso pre-made seasoning mixes do the trick, too. Add them as directed.

Place the buttered tortillas in a stack on top of the meat. Cover pan, and remove from heat. The steam from the cooked food will warm up the tortillas.

Once ready to serve, add refried beans, tomatoes, and cheese.

*Serve with:* Homemade or store-bought guacamole and tortilla chips. Guacamole is pretty easy to make, if you so desire: Combine 4 ripe avocados (cut into quarters, peeled, and pitted), 1 small red onion (diced), 1 clove of minced garlic, 1 tablespoon of lemon juice, 2 teaspoons of lime juice, and 1 jalapeño chile (optional) if you want to make it hot. Once ingredients are combined, cut up the avocado into small chunks, and add 1 medium tomato (chopped and seeded), before tossing and sprinkling on a dash of salt and pepper. For dessert, scoop up some raspberry sorbet, and make (or buy) a flourless chocolate cake. For a lighter option, you can whip up some Mexican hot chocolate—get Ibarra authentic Mexican chocolate (available in most specialty grocery stores). Heat whole milk in a saucepan over very low heat. Add two wedges of the chocolate for each cup of milk, and blend. Serve hot.

*The wine:* Forget straight-up red or white. For this meal, you need to make a pitcher of sangria. It's easy to make in advance and store in your fridge, and it's almost impossible to mess up. Combine 1 bottle of chilled red wine (Rioja, Cabernet, or Shiraz work best), 1/4 cup of brandy, 1/4 cup of triple sec, 2 tablespoons of sugar, 1 tablespoon of lime juice, a lemon and an orange, sliced thin. Refrigerate. Just before serving, add 1 cup of chilled seltzer and ice cubes.

*The music:* The *Buena Vista Social Club* soundtrack is perfect. Or anything by Silvio Rodriguez.

## Roast Night

After some deliberation, my mom decided to allow me to print her gravy recipe. No matter what else you might learn from this book, her gravy recipe alone is worth the price of admission. Cooking a roast for a man might conjure up memories of Sunday-night dinners from his childhood—and plant the seed of a future with you.

### Roast Beef with Vegetables

1 pound fresh green beans
1 (4-pound) sirloin steak roast
3 to 5 tablespoons self-rising flour
Salt and pepper, to taste
1 onion, peeled
1 jar onion juice
¼ cup beef stock (optional)
1 can Dawn Fresh mushroom steak sauce

A sirloin steak roast is best—it's very fatty, so it's the most flavorful, and shrinks down a lot while cooking. Also, it's harder to mess up than tenderloin or other lean cuts of beef.

Preheat the oven to 400 degrees Fahrenheit.

Set water to boil in a medium saucepan, and once boiling, add green beans. Cook 10 minutes. Meanwhile, remove all cellophane and paper from the roast (make sure you get that piece of cardboard or Styrofoam that's affixed to the bottom). Place the meat in a metal roasting pan.

Put 1 tablespoon of the flour in the pan, and sprinkle another on top of the roast. Season with salt and pepper. Place the onion in the pan. Pop it in the oven and cook, 20 minutes to the pound. When the roast is cooked through, set it on a plate.

*For the gravy:* Remove excess grease from the roasting pan, loosen the thickened juices with a fork, throw in the remaining flour (just a tablespoon or 2), and a little bit of the green-bean water to make a paste. As desired, add more liquid—use juice from vegetables, juice from a jar of onions, beef stock, Dawn Fresh mushroom steak sauce (my mom's secret ingredient). The key to flavorful gravy is to never use plain water, which dilutes the flavor rather than strengthens it.

*Serve with:* Mashed or roasted red potatoes and dinner rolls. For dessert, an apple, blueberry, or strawberry rhubarb pie with vanilla ice cream.

*The wine:* A rich Cabernet or Pinot Noir will complement the warm tones of this meal.

*The music:* Whatever most echoes your version of classic—be it Mozart, Ella Fitzgerald, or the Beatles.

# Art

That flawless dinner you cooked last night went off without a hitch. But now your man wants to take you out—to a museum, a play, a ballet, or an opera. Only trouble is, you don't know your baroque from your Baryshnikov. These next two sections will help you navigate the art of appreciating the arts.

## Museums

When I first took my little sister Caroline to Manhattan's finest art museums—the Met, MoMA, the Frick—she had only one question: how did all those volunteer curators (mostly middle-aged women in silk pashminas and understated makeup) support themselves? I told her what I have always believed to be true: those curators don't have to support themselves. They are the wives of extremely rich men.

A general knowledge of art is a must if you want to impress a cultured man. It shows him that you are worldly and smart, that you have an appreciation for beauty, and that you'll be able to hold your own around his family. In fact, when you express interest in, say, cubism, he is very likely to respond with, "How funny—my mother is a volunteer curator at the Guggenheim. You two should meet."

But what if, like me, you slept through one too many art history classes in college? What if the Met is just a beautiful building you pass on your way to Barneys? Fear not. Most museums have free nights every week, and it's perfectly acceptable to jump into any tour group while you're there. Listen carefully to what the curator says and ask questions about topics she mentions that interest you—Monet's use of light, say, or her son who works on Wall Street.

When visiting a museum with your man:

- **Skip the informational headset.** Those headsets that provide more detail than you'd ever need to know about an artist—from his use of color to his astrological sign to his childhood bed-wetting habit—may be interesting when you hit the museum with your grandmother. But when you're on a date they can detract from the point: getting to know each other. (They're also hazardous to your hair.) Instead, opt for a guided tour or (even better) buy the self-guided booklet so you can talk as you go.

- **Be aware of your surroundings.** Good manners are always a must, but in a museum they are even more crucial than usual. Keep your conversation at a low volume, remember to turn off your cell phone, don't stand too close to the artwork, and stay mindful of the pace of everyone around you. It's okay to linger over a painting that you love, just make sure you're not holding other people up.

- **Bypass the gift shop.** Nothing says "I never go to art museums" like a thirty-minute visit to an overpriced gift shop that ends with you asking your man to carry four of your eight new posters to dinner. If you really can't live without a Monet stationery set, go back the next weekend by yourself.

- **Bone up on the basics.** You don't have to be an expert, but it's good to have at least a general understanding of what you're looking at. If you plan on viewing a particular exhibit, you can check out the artist's work online ahead of time. If you're making a more general visit, here are the most common artistic periods, and the right names to drop:

**Renaissance (1300s):** Leonardo da Vinci, Michelangelo, Raphael

**Baroque (early 1600s):** Caravaggio, Rembrandt, Peter Paul Rubens, Diego Velázquez, Vermeer, Gianlorenzo Bernini

**Impressionism (1867):** Claude Monet, Pierre-Auguste Renoir, Camille Pissarro, Edgar Degas, Paul Cézanne, Edouard Manet, Mary Cassatt

**Fauvism (1905):** Henri Matisse, Albert Marquet, André Derain, Maurice de Vlaminck

**Cubism (1907):** Pablo Picasso, Marcel Duchamp, Georges Braque, Fernand Léger

**Abstract Expressionism (1940s–1960s):** Jackson Pollock, Mark Rothko, Franz Kline

**Postmodernism (1960–present):** Stephen McKenna, Carlo Maria Mariani, Peter Blake, David Hockney

## Opera, Theater, and Ballet

Perhaps these are three words that you've never associated with the practice of dating straight men. But in the course of interviewing wealthy guys for this book, I ran into quite a few who said that a woman's behavior at the opera, theater, or ballet speaks volumes about her breeding and manners. Here are the essentials for how to act.

**Dress up.** Modern etiquette does not dictate that you have to, but dress up anyway. If you are attending a matinee, wear a casual cotton skirt or dress. If you're going to an evening performance, aim for something a bit more formal. Nowadays, depending on where you live, anything goes when you're at a show. In London, lots of people wear jeans to the theater on Saturday night. But throwing on a skirt and heels shows that you care enough to make an effort.

**Be punctual.** There are always a few stragglers at any performance—those people lurking guiltily in the shadows until the end of Act I. Don't be one of them. Make sure that you are at the theater, with tickets in hand, at least twenty minutes before the show starts. This means that if you are picking up tickets at the box office, you should be half an hour early. If by some chance you do arrive late, it's up to the usher to decide when to allow you in. You might get to sneak to your seats after the overture, but you may have to wait even longer. Be polite and don't argue with him. And next time, get there early.

**Shut up.** Once the lights go down in a theater, even the most refined adults sometimes start to act like kids at a boring school assembly. They shift in their seats, they unwrap cough drops, they flip through their programs, they whisper to their husbands, "Wasn't he on *CSI: Miami* last week? No, no. Not him. The one playing Orlando." It's essential to be silent while watching a play, ballet, or opera. Make sure your phone is turned off, keep your hands in your lap, don't get up to go to the bathroom, and don't open your mouth until intermission. And when you see musicals, don't ever sing along. I don't care if *Oklahoma!* is your all-time favorite show and you know every word to "Surrey with the Fringe on Top." You're at the theater, not a Kelly Clarkson concert, so behave.

**Applause.** As they say before TV cop shows, viewer discretion is advised. There's no need for you to be the loudest clapper in the auditorium—or the first. In general, applause occurs at the end of every act, and sometimes at the end of a major dance number, scene, or aria. During a classical music concert, it's important not to clap until the piece is over. Clapping between movements is not allowed or expected. If you're not sure whether to clap at any given moment, wait to see what everyone else does. Clapping is polite, and standing ovations at the show's end (though far too commonly done these days) are fine. But never, ever scream or whistle to signify your enjoyment unless you are at a football game. If the spirit moves you at the opera, you can yell out "Bravo!" (for a male performer), "Brava!" (for a female), or "Bravi!" (for two or more performers).

**Making an exit.** Unless the theater is on fire, there is no excuse for leaving your seat until the house lights come up. That's all there is to say about that.

## Dude Movies for a Million, Alex

Wealth aside for a moment, here's an important lesson to learn: contrary to what many women believe, men don't find it endearing that you've never seen their favorite movies. One way to separate yourself from the pack is to start up a conversation about which of the *Rocky* flicks was the best or how you just can't get enough of watching Kevin Costner play baseball. This worked well for a friend of mine when we went with a group of four English (and, incidentally, quite wealthy) guys to see *Kill Bill.* As we were walking out of the theater, I gave my standard "too much blood, too many women in spandex" comment. My friend, however, busted out a full review of all the Japanese directors Tarantino paid homage to, and the next day, I kid you not, three of those guys called to ask her out. The only one who didn't was my boyfriend, and he probably would have done the same if he hadn't been on a Meryl Streep-a-thon lockdown in our apartment. Hey, they should experience our movies, too.

So if you think *Full Metal Jacket* is just a strangely uncomfortable fashion choice, or you don't know your *Swingers* from your *Swing Kids,* I'd suggest stocking up on the popcorn. Here's a list of the dude movies you must see (feel free to alternate viewings with Meg Ryan flicks as necessary).

The *Alien* franchise

*Anchorman* and *Old School*

*Apocalypse Now*

*The Big Lebowski* and *Fargo*

*Caddyshack*

*Clerks*

*Cool Hand Luke*

*Die Hard I–III*

*Diner*

*Donnie Darko*

*The Exorcist*

*Full Metal Jacket*

*Gladiator*

*Godfather I* and *II*
(The third one is awful. He will appreciate your powers of discernment.)

*Goodfellas*

*The Great Escape*

*Heat*

*Major League*

*Monty Python and the Holy Grail* (or any Monty Python movie, for that matter)

*Natural Born Killers*

*The Natural*

*Patton*

*Pulp Fiction*

*Raging Bull*

*Rebel Without a Cause*

*Rocky I–V*

*Rounders*

*Saving Private Ryan*

*Scarface*

*Seven*

*The Shawshank Redemption*

*The Shining*

*Snatch*

*Swingers*

*This Is Spinal Tap*

*Taxi Driver*

*Terminator I* and *II*

*Top Gun*

*Unforgiven*

*The Usual Suspects*

## Take Me Out to the Ball Game

In much the same way that men—regardless of how wealthy they are—like it when you've seen their favorite films, they also appreciate a woman who knows at least a little bit about sports. When I interviewed guys on this topic, almost all of them said that they like going to games on dates, but can't stand it when a woman asks tons of obvious questions about what the players are doing. Even worse are the women who go, but just act bored out of their minds the entire time. One lawyer friend of mine told me that he brought a girl from his office to a Mets game on their second date. "For the first few innings, she just talked to a friend on the phone," he said. "Then she finally hung up, and I was relieved for about five seconds—until she pulled a little bottle from out of her purse and started painting her nails."

Yikes.

Remember that sporting events, in addition to being a hobby and a pleasure for some men, are also the backdrop for a lot of business meetings (both yours and his). You don't want your man picturing you giving yourself a manicure in his boss's luxury box. If he does, you can consider the game over.

I don't want to stereotype here, because I know plenty of women who love sports. But I, for one, do not. I didn't even like Sporty Spice. I used to be the girl who went to the basketball game, cheered loudly, and then on the drive home asked, "So, who won?" Over the years, I have learned how to feign interest while watching sports (and sometimes I am actually interested . . .). Here's the cheat sheet for those of you who are similarly clueless. But don't worry if you can't bring yourself to memorize (or even read) it. Just be enthusiastic, and try to have fun. (Remember: where there's a sporting event, there is pizza and beer. Or at least cuddling on the couch while you watch ESPN.)

## Basketball: The Basics

The National Basketball Association (NBA) is divided into two conferences, Eastern and Western. Each team has twelve players who rotate throughout the game—five players on the court at a time. Basketball season lasts from October through June, at which point the winning team in each conference competes in the NBA Finals. Just like your sorority scavenger hunts in college, the team with the most points wins. Teams face off for twelve-minute quarters (no, you won't be out of the arena in less time than it takes to watch an episode of *The Sopranos*—because of time-outs, the average game lasts for about two and a half hours). Baskets (or field goals) are worth either two or three points, depending on whether they're shot from behind or in front of the painted arcs at either end of the court (called the three-point line). Penalty free throws are worth one point each. Players must dribble (bounce the ball with one hand) while running, and—unlike in your sorority scavenger hunt—they are not allowed to hold, trip, hit, or push. If the game ends in a tie, overtime periods of five minutes each are played until one team scores the most points.

## Basketball: The Guy

While other sports fans are known to worship their sport of choice with a clicker and a bag of Cheetos, the basketball fan tends to actually *play* as well as watch. Thus, he is your best bet if you're looking for someone fit.

Pro basketball teams play several times a week, but they get a lot less television airtime than football or baseball games. Translation: you can feign interest in his favorite team without devoting several Saturdays a year to it.

## Baseball: The Game

Major League Baseball teams are divided into two groups: the National League and the American League. At the end of every season (April through October) the pennant winners of each league compete in the World Series. Baseball is known as the great American pastime for good reason—you can pass some serious time watching a game, since there's no limit to the length (though most are over in about two and a half hours). A game consists of nine innings (like basketball, if the game is tied at the end they keep playing), each one split into *the top,* when the visiting team is at bat and the home team is in the field, and *the bottom,* when they switch positions. Each batter gets three strikes before he's out. The object of the game is to score as many runs (a run is a completion of all the bases) as possible. Batters hit either a single (running to first base), a double (running to second), a triple (running to third), or a home run (making it around all the bases and back to home plate). The opposing team mans the field and tries to tag the base runners out before they make it to home plate.

## Baseball: The Guy

Baseball is often referred to as the thinking man's sport, but all those extra IQ points might be wasted on an encyclopedic knowledge of statistics and scores. Each team in the Major Leagues plays an average of six games a week, so if he's truly devoted, you may be spending a lot of nights on the couch—or getting him a TiVo for his birthday.

## Football: The Game

Pro football can be a little intimidating if you didn't grow up watching it every Sunday (ahem, thanks, Dad). The National Football League (NFL) is broken into two conferences: the American Football Conference and the National Football Conference. Football season begins in September and lasts until the beginning of the following year, at which point the winning teams from each conference compete in the Superbowl. A football game is broken into fifteen-minute quarters—but, as I learned as a little kid while fighting for the remote, it lasts a lot longer than an hour because of time-outs. Think three times as long.

There are two teams in a football game: offense and defense. The offense's goal is to carry the football across the other team's goal line (and into the end zone). The offense gets four downs (or chances) to advance the ball ten yards. If they don't succeed, it's the other team's turn. The defensive team tries to stop this from happening by catching the ball mid-pass (called an interception) or by causing the offense to drop the ball (called a fumble). The team with the most points wins. If a game is tied at the end of the fourth quarter, teams play one fifteen-minute overtime (called "sudden death"). If it's still tied after that, don't worry: the game ends in a tie and you can start watching reruns of *The Golden Girls.*

## Football: The Guy

The good news is that each team in pro football plays only one game a week. The bad news is that this gives the football guy six days to get pumped and talk endlessly about strategy (you will become intimately familiar with the term "Monday morning quarterback"). A real football fan is relentlessly faithful to his team, his friends, and (bonus!) the woman in his life.

Football, basketball, and baseball are the sports most often watched by the masses—both on TV and in person. But certain athletic activities hold even more appeal for wealthy, cultured men (namely the sports that they might have played in prep school, and at which fans are more likely to be covered in Polo than in body paint). You might want to consider brushing up on one or more of the following, because you may be called on to watch—or even play—them over the course of your relationship.

- Golf
- Tennis
- Sailing
- Skiing
- Soccer
- Squash
- Lacrosse

## SECRET WEAPON: Fantasy Sports

The following is a lesson in adaptation. And (sort of) in sportiness.

Recently I was out with several guys who were complaining that the women in their lives cannot begin to understand the importance of fantasy sports. When I mentioned that I am on an all-girls fantasy baseball team and that I fully understood when my boyfriend canceled dinner one Saturday night because his fantasy football draft had been going on for twelve hours and was nowhere near done, these guys looked at me like I was Angelina Jolie in a string bikini.

But, as I went on to explain to them, a year ago I would have thought fantasy sports were immature, stupid, and a waste of time. My good friend Caitlin (who is actually sporty) decided to start an all-girls fantasy baseball league, and I got dragged into it. For those of you who don't know what fantasy sports are all about, here's the rundown: You and a bunch of other people form a league and you draft the best players from different teams, forming a sort of superteam. You input all your players into a form on Yahoo! (go to http://fantasysports.yahoo.com/) and the Internet does the rest. Each time one of your players scores in a real-life game, the results of his singular actions are tallied and put toward your team's total results. If you've been living under a rock or in a cloistered convent for the last few years, here's a piece of advice: men are insane about fantasy sports.

I am the consummate girly girl. I practically have the color pink radiating off of me. So when Caitlin announced that she was forming a fantasy league, I pretty much planned to phone it in and just pick a team of guys who all had the last name Smith. But then I was fully introduced to the wonderful world of fantasy sports online. You can view every player's photo, stats, and ranking (incidentally, if you want to date a professional athlete, this is also a great place to check men out). I was hooked. Never in my life have I experienced something so close to my favorite childhood occupation—playing Barbies. When I was a kid, I had over a hundred Barbie dolls. When all the girls in the neighborhood would come over to play (there were about ten of us in all), we'd lay the Barbies out in rows, and take turns picking the ones we wanted. I was the master of this. Not only did I always get the best dolls, I devised ways of convincing the other girls that they wanted the crappier ones (mostly by talking them up, even though I myself had no interest in them). This was the exact strategy I used during my fantasy draft, and it worked.

In fantasy baseball, there are three categories that matter: speed, power, and average. If you've got Johnny Damon and Jose Reyes to cover you on speed, and then, say, Giambi and Piazza to score runs, you're golden. For average, you need someone who has the total package, plus some extra, wild-card sort of qualities. In Barbies, there are likewise three categories: hot Barbies like Skipper and Malibu Barbie (speed), Barbies who actually do things, like lawyer or veterinarian Barbie (power), and Barbies who have extras, such as Heart Family Barbie, who's otherwise quite lame, but comes with a four-door sedan and two babies (average). To get the perfect mix in a game of Barbies, you need some of each. Likewise with the fantasy baseball.

My fantasy team ranked in the top three all season long, even though I know nothing about sports. In part because of my Barbie-inspired drafting style, but in part because of my obsession with my players. I've realized that while women everywhere are killing time at work by e-mailing men and then obsessing about why it's taking them more than thirty-seven minutes to reply, men are killing time by checking their stats on Yahoo! Apparently, the average guy does this ten to twenty times a day. And now, so do I. It's just as addictive as overanalyzing relationships, and you can actually make money at it.

Most women look at fantasy sports as some alien occupation that only men or super-sporty chicks can get into. But in fact, they appeal to even the girliest of girls. Why am I going on about this? Because sometimes when we talk to men, it seems like we're whispering at each other in two different languages from opposite sides of the Grand Canyon: *You're thirty years old, and you're actually pouting over the results of a football game? You've got to be kidding me.* But maybe we're not so different. Maybe we just need a translator. If fantasy baseball is like playing Barbies and gossiping (which it totally is), then I'm a fan.

It's important to stretch your boundaries and give him a little credit. If some guy had introduced me to fantasy baseball, you can bet I would have laughed it off as a stupid, puerile activity. But because it was my friend Caitlin, I actually gave it a chance, and fell in love. Keep an open mind about his interests. And in the meantime, get some girlfriends together and start a fantasy league. In addition to being fun, it will send any man you meet into an absolute tizzy. Here's how to do it:

**Pick a sport.** The most popular fantasy sports are the most popular pro sports, and since they're played based on actual games, the fantasy season coincides directly with the real season. Throughout the year, you can create leagues for football, baseball, basketball, and hockey, as well as more random sports like cricket and NASCAR. If you search hard enough, you can probably even throw together a fantasy mini-golf league. Extra points for knowing the circumference of the clown's mouth and the relative speed of the windmill.

**Generate interest.** Your female friends might not be immediately sold on the idea, so do what Caitlin did to us—incorporate league rules that have nothing whatsoever to do with sports. In our league, every team had a theme song (or, in my case, every player had his own Frank Sinatra song), a general theme (like hot guys, fat guys, guys with facial hair . . .), and a hilarious name (wish I'd been the one to think up Sandy Cohen's Eyebrows—and would love to see that printed on a jersey). Caitlin also threw a fabulous draft party, complete with a bucket full of pink cosmos.

**Create the league and get everyone else to join.** Go to http://fantasysports.yahoo.com/. Click on "Start a League," and follow the directions for setting up teams and drafting players. Once you've drafted players in person, someone will have to enter everyone's lineups online—or each individual can enter her own team to save time.

**Do your research.** There are many tools at your disposal. First and foremost: men. Ask the guys at work, in your social circle, and at bars and parties to help you out (even if you already know which players you want). I am the queen of striking up conversations with men, and I can tell you that this is the most successful method of doing so that I have ever used. Talking about fantasy sports puts men at ease, and separates you out from the dozens of other women asking, "So, where are you from? What do you do?" Yahoo! has a list of all available fantasy players, ranked in relation to the entire league and by position. And there are actually fantasy sports periodicals available at your local newsstand, or from the lending library of your latest crush.

**Shamelessly use your newfound knowledge to meet men.** When Caitlin started our fantasy league, she had no intention of using it as a tool for meeting men. However, she recognized even before I did that I would exploit it for that purpose faster than you can say "home run." From the time you draft until after the Series, you have one fabulous pick-up line at your disposal. Last spring, my girlfriends rolled their eyes each time we went into a bar, and I propped myself next to the cutest guy with his eyes on the TV screen. "How's Santana doing?" I'd ask. And when he smiled at me, I'd say, "He's on my fantasy team." Oh, who cares if it's a little manipulative? It works.

## Volunteering

If you can pull yourself away from your fantasy team for a few spare hours a week, here's a suggestion that will benefit others and improve your chances of meeting Mr. Right simultaneously. Start volunteering. A lot of quality rich men were raised by mothers who did charity work. They also probably had to put in service hours in prep school. A lot of them never broke the habit. One of my best friends wanted a dog, but her fabulous rent-controlled building didn't allow pets. She decided to walk shelter dogs instead and got a volunteer position through the ASPCA. On her second day of training, she met her now fiancé, a real estate attorney whose mother had been telling him for years about the organization's great volunteer program (she's on the board, naturally).

Need I say more?

Go to www.idealist.org to find out what kind of volunteer work suits you best.

## Required Reading

Once you meet that great guy on your weekly Habitat for Humanity shift, he'll probably want to introduce you to his friends. A quality man's partner needs to be able to discuss major works of literature as comfortably as she can discuss the most recent episode of *The Office.* Here's a list of books that the educated class likes to refer to in casual conversation. In no way is this a comprehensive list (read Harold Bloom's *Canon* if you want that). These titles range from obscure (and therefore important and impressive) to so damn obvious that PBS has made at least three miniseries out of them. Perhaps your Norton anthologies from college are still gathering dust under your bed in your parents' house. Or perhaps you've spent more time with *Cosmo* than with Camus recently. Don't worry. Here's what to say if one of these classics comes up and you haven't read it (or don't remember it—hey, it's been a while since freshman lit). In case of emergency, excuse yourself from the conversation, run into the other room, and check out www.pinkmonkey.com.

You'll thank me later.

- ***The Decameron* by Giovanni Boccaccio.** Like Dante's *Divine Comedy.* But funny.

- ***The Canterbury Tales* by Geoffrey Chaucer.** Farting jokes, cuckolded husbands, and bawdy women on horseback. Basically the *Old School* of the Middle Ages.

- ***Paradise Lost* by John Milton.** In keeping with its Garden of Eden theme, the text commits a sin of its own by causing indescribable waves of boredom to wash over the reader.

- **Anything by Shakespeare.** There's a lot of ground to cover here, so I suggest familiarizing yourself with one comedy, one tragedy, and a couple of sonnets. That way when someone wants to discuss a Shakespearean play that you don't know, you can just say "I vastly prefer [insert whichever one you know here]."

- **Anything by Jane Austen.** Why? Because every cultured man loves a woman who knows her *Northanger Abbey* from her *Sense and Sensibility.* Plus, Austen pokes fun at women who try to snag rich men at all costs, and rewards those who look for both money and love. Which is why, back in the Smith College English department, we had a motto: *WWJAD: What Would Jane Austen Do?*

- ***Bleak House* by Charles Dickens.** The first book to be sold in serialized form. HBO learned everything they know from Dickens.

- *Moby-Dick* **by Herman Melville.** Just mention Ishmael setting sail from Nantucket, and hope that sends him into a diatribe about how Martha's Vineyard is the far superior of the two islands.

- *The Scarlet Letter* **by Nathaniel Hawthorne.** Resist the urge to make a Demi Moore reference.

- *Heart of Darkness* **by Joseph Conrad.** By all means, make an *Apocalypse Now* reference.

- *Les Miserables* **by Victor Hugo.** If you know all the words to "Castle on a Cloud," you're money.

- *The Mill on the Floss* **by George Eliot.** Just shake your head, laugh, and say "Truly, the most befuddling ending in all of literature."

- *Pale Fire* **by Vladimir Nabokov.** Say "You have to admire the use of an unreliable narrator."

- *The Catcher in the Rye* **by J. D. Salinger.** You probably won't have to say anything. Just nod knowingly as he compares the book to his freshman year at Choate.

- *The Stranger* **by Albert Camus.** Let him know that the Cure's "Killing an Arab" was inspired by this book.

- *Of Mice and Men* **by John Steinbeck.** Giving new meaning to the phrase "I didn't know my own strength," Lennie accidentally kills a puppy and his boss's wife. Proving once again that size does matter.

- ***Atlas Shrugged*** **by Ayn Rand.** Describe it as "heavy." You'll mean that the damn thing weighs seven pounds. He'll think you're referring to the plot.

- ***The Sound and the Fury*** **by William Faulkner.** If he's from the South, change the subject. If not, just say "And I thought my family was dysfunctional . . ."

- ***A Farewell to Arms*** **by Ernest Hemingway.** A tragic love story set against the backdrop of war. So engrossing, so captivating, and yet—when Henry proposes and his girlfriend Catherine says, "How could we be more married?"—clearly, a work of fiction (written by a man).

- ***The Bonfire of the Vanities*** **by Tom Wolfe.** A satire of status-crazy New York in the 1980s from the ultimate social commentator/novelist since F. Scott Fitzgerlad.

- ***A Heartbreaking Work of Staggering Genius*** **by Dave Eggers.** Or as a British friend of mine calls it, a heartbreaking work of staggering pomposity. Eggers, the founder of the hip and offbeat literary journal *McSweeney's,* shows that he is no different from most young men—he can talk about himself for hours. And hours. And hours.

While we're on the topic of reading, an easy and inexpensive way to stay updated on current events and culture is to subscribe to at least one Sunday paper. The *New York Times* is your best bet, and can safely be called a girl's (second) best friend. I know women who've landed great husbands after they whispered over espresso that they love nothing more than to spend their Sundays curled up with the *Times* and a cup of coffee, even if they do start with the Style section.

I'd also suggest getting at least one additional (and educational) magazine subscription, on any topic that you want to learn more about. And by any topic, I don't mean makeup or celebrity gossip. I mean a topic that will impress the sort of guy you want to marry. Think about it this way: if you read it, he will come.

- **Food and wine:** *Wine Spectator, Gourmet, Bon Appetit*
- **Politics:** *The Economist*
- **Sports:** *Sports Illustrated*
- **Travel:** *Condé Nast Traveler, National Geographic*
- **Art:** *Art Forum*
- **Culture, current events, and literature:** *Harper's, The Atlantic Monthly, The New Yorker*
- **General trivia and facts:** *Mental Floss*

## Man-Proofing Your Apartment

You're almost ready. You know what to wear, what to say, and what to cook for dinner. But before you meet Mr. Wonderful and invite him over for a romantic evening, you're gonna need to man-proof your home. My Aunt Nancy told me that the first thing she did when she started getting serious with her then-boyfriend (now-husband) was upgrade her cable package so that she'd have access to all the major sports networks. I recently asked my uncle what he saw in her in those early months and without skipping a beat, he said, "We used to have so much fun sitting around at her apartment, watching TV and talking. It was just so comfortable." Yup, and the ESPN 2 didn't hurt either.

A man's home may be his castle, but putting him at ease in your home might just be the key to cohabitation. Some other things to bear in mind:

**Keep a six-pack of beer in your fridge.** All men like beer. Men of a certain social status are rather discerning (read: snobby) about the brands they prefer. You'll impress with any of the following: For foreign beers, go with Heineken, Stella Artois, or Hoegaarden. For domestics, go with Sierra Nevada, Magic Hat, or Sam Adams. The men I asked about this surprised me when they said (unanimously) that they'd find it odd if a woman had tons of obscure varieties of beer hanging around. So don't worry about trying too hard. Basically, as one of them put it, "If she has something for me to drink that isn't Smirnoff Ice or Mike's Hard Whatever, then I'll be happy."

**Invest in video games.** I am in no way above improving my apartment just for the sake of a man. However, when my sister gave me the old-school Nintendo NES last Christmas, impressing dudes with it was the last thing on my mind. I came *thisclose* to quitting my job, just so I'd have more free time to play Super Mario 3. But a fabulous side effect of owning Nintendo is that every male who enters my apartment is instantly tempted to take up permanent residence on the couch. If you have any desire whatsoever to have video games (or men by the droves) at your place, buy an Xbox, PlayStation, or Game Cube immediately.

**Hide the stuffed animals.** Though you may still find all eight of your original Cabbage Patch dolls just as lovable as ever, they could cause the man in your life to get an acute case of the creepy-crawlies. Some women tend to accumulate toys and dolls and teddy bears over the years. I would never tell you to get rid of any of these things, especially if they have sentimental value. Just find a new place for them. Like in the back of your closet or under the bed.

**Make the place comfortable.** Though many of us conjure up images of the typical man's apartment as dirty and underdecorated and the typical woman's apartment as pristine and pink, I have never seen these distinctions play out in real life. Modern women are busy with work and friends, and those of us who live in urban shoeboxes don't tend to entertain all that much anyway. But when you invite a man over (especially early on in the relationship), prepare in the same way that you would if you were having out-of-town guests. Make sure you have enough of the essentials—toilet paper, milk, fresh water, clean bath towels. Don't leave the sink full of dishes, or the garbage overflowing. And don't assume that just because he's a guy, he won't notice if your place is a mess. Even if it's subconscious, he will be assessing what it would be like to live with you in the future by how you live now.

**Clean your bathroom.** I interviewed a dozen or so guys for a magazine piece about what happens when couples move in together. As one of them put it, "The bathroom is just one big hairball. I never knew my girlfriend had that much hair, and frankly, it scares me." Be considerate and clean up after yourself in the bathroom when he's coming over (and that goes double for when you use *his* bathroom).

## Knowing It All

This chapter was meant to provide you with information and cheat sheets on a lot of important topics—important in general, but even more so when it comes to dating. It's great for you to know a little bit (or a lot) about sports, wine, art, movies, and the like. But just remember: nobody can know it all. Sometimes it seems that we are programmed to always have an answer to every question. But if you haven't read the book he's talking about, or been to his favorite new restaurant, it's okay to admit it. Part of the fun of meeting someone new who is your intellectual and economic equal is that you will have a chance to learn from one another.

# Go Out and Find Him

"There certainly are not so many men of large fortune in the world as there are pretty women to deserve them."

—Jane Austen, *Mansfield Park*

My uncle used to tell a joke about a guy named Bob who desperately wanted to win the lottery. Night after night, he would kneel down beside his bed and plead: "Dear God, please let me win tomorrow." The next morning he'd check the winning numbers, and sigh with disappointment. This went on for days, weeks, months, until one night, Bob shouted: "*Please,* God, just give me this one thing! Let me win the lottery and I'll never ask you to answer another prayer as long as I live."

A moment later, he heard a voice: "Bob, this is God. I've heard your prayers and I want to help you—but do you think you could meet me halfway and buy a ticket?"

If you want to win the quality man lottery, you're going to have to buy a ticket, which means leaving your apartment and going where the boys are. In this chapter you'll learn how and where to find the quality man of your dreams, and what to say to make sure he'll call.

But first, let's examine who's out there.

## The Nine Most Common Types of Rich Men

Not all rich men are created equal. Perhaps you desire a husband who will take you on lavish trips (even if he is a little too show-offy), or perhaps you want one who has an incredible work ethic (even if it means you see him for only two hours a week). No man is without his flaws, but it is possible to gauge just who you're dealing with (and just how wealthy he is) based on your very first interaction if you know what clues to look for. Most rich men, good or bad, fall into one of the following categories:

### The Worker Bee

*Education:* He may have attended an Ivy League college or graduate school, but he was a public school kid until then.

*Occupation:* He works eighty-hour weeks at a major corporate law firm / investment bank / private, university-affiliated hospital.

*Never seen without:* His BlackBerry.

*Real estate:* His apartment is in an A-list building, but he still sleeps on a futon and uses milk crates as bookshelves.

*Fitness routine:* Not one to blow his hard-earned money on an expensive gym membership, he runs in the park for exercise before work (at around five a.m.), and does push-ups and sit-ups in his bedroom, while listening to Journey's greatest hits.

*Vacation destination:* He does not take vacations, but dreams of going camping with his college buddies when he next gets a week off—probably in 2009. A few weekends a year you'll find him in Las Vegas, attending a bachelor party.

*His opening line:* "Hi, can I buy you a— Oh, shit, that's my office calling. I'm just going to step outside and take this. Be right back."

*Pros and cons:* The Worker Bee has a lot going for him. He's well-bred, but he wasn't raised with money, so he isn't pretentious. He's close to his family, and they are down-to-earth and super-proud of their boy. Money is not the main event for him, so he won't use it to try to impress you, but he will take you out for nice dinners and give great if slightly practical presents (cameras, DVD players, etc. This guy is more Best Buy than Bergdorf's). The Worker Bee is the perfect mate for any woman who doesn't mind being alone a lot. Maybe you're busy at work yourself and can't imagine fitting a full-time relationship into your schedule, or maybe you just prefer spending Saturday nights out with your girlfriends. In any case, you'll be putting the me back in me-time if you end up with this guy, so be prepared. And don't even think about complaining about his late hours. The Worker Bee hates feeling guilty and needs a woman who supports his work ethic.

*Future prediction:* Your first fight as man and wife will occur on your honeymoon, when he insists on calling the office twice a day. You'll have a huge house (probably in a suburb of the major city where you met), and you will call all the shots on how it should be decorated. If you don't want to work, he'll be fine with that, so long as you do something productive with your time; he won't approve of your sitting around all day watching *Oprah.* You'll cry when he misses your firstborn's first steps, but you'll smile happily as he writes the check that sends her off to college loan-free.

### The Foreigner

*Education:* Probably attended one of Europe's most prestigious universities, but he'll never say for sure. Don't try to impress him by saying you went to William and Mary—he'll think it's a major department store.

*Occupation:* The Foreigner occupies himself with leisure. In New York, you'll find him lounging outside of Pastis at three o'clock on Tuesday. In other parts of the country, he's that tall, dark, and handsome man reading in the coffee shop mid-afternoon as you rush in to get your boss a latte. Look for capri pants and sandals. That'll be him.

*Never seen without:* His brand-new sports car. He might not be able to remember what he did last week, but he can rattle off every one of that car's special features in sixty seconds or less.

*Real estate:* His family owns buildings all over town, and he keeps apartments in at least three of them.

*Fitness routine:* He meditates or takes long, thoughtful walks at night. He won't, under any circumstances, sweat just to burn calories.

*Vacation destination:* His parents' vineyards in Australia, his grandfather's second home on the Amalfi Coast, his uncle's beach house in Greece. Be prepared to see some amazing sights—and to spend a lot of time with his extended family.

*His opening line:* "In my country, we have a word to describe beauty like yours . . ."

*Pros and cons:* His sexy accent, romantic nature and thoughtful gifts (read: expensive jewelry) will touch your heart. But you'll be annoyed when you have to explain what *The Brady Bunch* is for the seventy-third time.

*Future prediction:* When he eventually grows up and takes over his share of the family business, you'll be free to kick back and raise the kids if you so desire. Your children will have lyrical names that mean something in Spanish/French/Italian/Portugese. You will fight about whose homeland to settle in, and strike a compromise by purchasing estates in both countries. You're nothing if not flexible.

### The Politician

*Education:* Harvard or Yale.

*Occupation:* Whether he's running for school board or Congress, this man is equally occupied by his political agenda and his unmarred reputation.

*Never seen without:* An entourage of people making sure that the aforementioned reputation remains unmarred.

*Real estate:* He bought his first home at the age of twenty-four with family money. However, as the story goes, he saved up to buy it, and (so eager is he to raise a solid American family) he bought a stuffed elephant/donkey for his first-born's bedroom before he even had a serious girlfriend.

*Fitness routine:* Jogs along his city/town's busiest thoroughfare so he can wave to his constituents as he goes.

*Vacation destination:* His parents' beach house (in the most expensive area of his home state).

*His opening line:* "What district do you vote in?"

*Pros and cons:* The politician is passionate about his career, and part of that is building a solid family, so you'll never have to convince him to get married. That said, if you want him to marry you, you can kiss Friday-night tequila shots and bar dancing good-bye.

*Future prediction:* His convictions will impress and inspire you, but your home will be a revolving door of managers, journalists, and supporters with picket signs. You will have at least four children, and your job will go the way of those tequila shots when you dedicate your entire life to the campaign.

## The Artist

*Education:* Either an impressive conservatory like Juilliard or the Sorbonne, or the School of Lucky Breaks.

*Occupation:* A rare breed, the successful self-made artist comes in many forms—actor, painter, musician, photographer, writer . . .

*Never seen without:* His pain.

*Real estate:* Usually involves a loft of some kind, and a studio space in case he gets inspired in the middle of the night.

*Fitness routine:* None—unless he's an actor. In that case, he works out two to three times a day, and consumes a sickening amount of egg whites and protein shakes.

*Vacation destination:* The great museums of Europe. Don't worry, you can shop in London/Paris/Florence/Rome, too.

*His opening line:* "I'd love to show you some of my work sometime."

*Pros and cons:* His talent (and the fact that he supports himself by doing what he loves) will make you head over heels. His overemotional nature will make you want to write a letter of apology to every ex-boyfriend you yelled at for never talking about his feelings.

*Future prediction:* Being the wife of a successful artist will expose you to a world of culture and excitement you never knew. You will meet all the major players on the art scene and attend the best parties and gallery openings. You'll seethe when he says that he thinks having children is just a selfish attempt at immortality, while he simultaneously clutters your town house with his new collection of self-portraits.

## New Moneybags

*Education:* Any one of several small liberal arts colleges—Bates, Bennington, Middlebury, Pomona, Williams, Amherst, Harvey Mudd, etc.

*Occupation:* A New Moneybags man comes in all varieties. If he's not a banker or a founding VP of a successful Internet company, you usually can't pin down exactly *what* he does—he'll say he's a consultant, a venture capitalist, a trader, or an investor.

*Real estate:* Hip downtown apartment in the hippest of downtown buildings. Fully furnished by his personal decorator, and cleaned twice a week by a housekeeper who also works as a model/C-list actress. Note the surround-sound speakers and new plasma TV.

*Never seen without:* The hottest new cell phone. You know, the one that's the size of a thimble, but can take pictures, record music, and cook a seven-course dinner.

*Fitness routine:* Whether or not he ever actually goes there, he's a member at the most exclusive gym in town.

*Vacation destination:* St. Tropez, Palm Beach, Southampton.

*His opening line:* "Didn't I meet you at that movie premiere after-party at Soho House last month?"

*Pros and cons:* The New Moneybags can be a fun date if you're willing to overlook the shameless name-dropping, countless shopping excursions to Thomas Pink, and his tendency to be more beautifully groomed than you are. As a husband, you may find him exasperating at times, but he will take you to all the best restaurants, parties, and openings.

*Future prediction:* Your wedding will appear in a *Town & Country* spread. You'll live in New York or LA in an apartment full of African art and sleek chrome surfaces. You'll argue about whether you need a third Porsche convertible, and about why a baby should ever wear Burberry. But as long as he keeps making the money he needs to maintain such a flashy lifestyle (and as long as you keep a steady supply of earplugs on hand), you'll be happy.

## Old Moneybags (Working)

*Education:* Dartmouth or Princeton, preceded by a distinguished prep school where his father, grandfather, and great-grandfather all played football. If you overhear him waxing nostalgic about Choate or Andover, you'll know you've probably got an Old Moneybags on your hands.

*Occupation:* He's a lawyer or banker in the same firm where his father (now a partner) started out.

*Never seen without:* His father's Harvard tie.

*Real estate:* Sprawling yet understated apartment, decorated by Mom. Expect to see at least one Oriental rug and a wall of yellowing family photos in frames.

*Fitness routine:* Regularly plays squash and tennis. Golfs once a week with his dad and brothers. Currently training for his fourth marathon.

*Vacation destination:* The family cabin on Lake Winnipesaukee. They'll call it "camp," but it will have a full staff, heated swimming pool, and eight bedrooms. If he's truly Old Wasp, don't expect cable TV.

*His opening line:* "I see you're having a gin and tonic. My mother's favorite drink."

*Pros and Cons:* His money, like his family name, is as solid as it comes. He's been raised in a sophisticated home and has impeccable manners, but his sense of entitlement and inability to empathize with those less fortunate will grate on you at times. You will have to convince his mother that you're worthy.

*Future prediction:* He will take you to Nantucket for a long weekend and propose with his great-grandma's six-carat ring. Life will be just peachy as long as you stay in his mother's good graces. He will want to send your kids off to summer camp pretty much as soon as they start walking, and you'll have to tread lightly when discussing prep school.

## Old Moneybags (Inheritance)

*Education:* See Old Moneybags (Working).

*Occupation:* None. Or one of several artistic variations on none, such as unpublished novelist/singer, painter/photographer, or screenwriter/tango instructor.

*Never seen without:* Daddy's credit card.

*Real estate:* For now he's living in one of his parents' spare classic six apartments. Once he meets the right girl, though, there's a place off Park Avenue that he's had his eye on for years.

*Fitness routine:* Mid-afternoon yoga classes.

*Vacation destination:* Africa, Thailand, Budapest. He loves adventure travel and Buddhist retreats, and never resists the urge to put down his gold AmEx someplace new.

*His closing line:* "I almost forgot— Would you like to go to Paris with me tomorrow?"

*Pros and cons:* Since he's not working, he'll have plenty of time to hang out with you. However, he won't understand when you have a deadline at work. If you complain about your boss he'll say, "Why don't you just quit?" The perfect man for a woman who wants to know someone's at home watching the kids while she's at the office, or for the woman who wants nothing more from life than to see the world with her carefree husband.

*Future prediction:* He'll convince you to take the summer off and travel across Europe with him, all expenses paid. He will age beautifully, thanks to his stress-free existence and twice-yearly Botox injections, and he will make you laugh until you're old and gray, but you'll stay up nights wondering exactly why it is that he's content to do nothing. You'll cringe when your kid comes home from career day at school and asks, "Daddy, what's *your* career?" Be ready for a major mid-life What-Do-I-Have-to-Show-for-Myself meltdown.

## Old Southern Moneybags

*Education:* Four years (or maybe five) at one of the best institutions south of the Mason-Dixon line. Possibly Vanderbilt, Rice, Baylor, Ole Miss, or the University of Virginia.

*Occupation:* Vice president of his family business, a major tobacco conglomerate.

*Never seen without:* A jacket and collared shirt. This guy doesn't do casual.

*Real estate:* A palatial home with acres and acres of land. Do not, under any circumstances, call it a plantation.

*Fitness routine:* Touch football with his college buddies every Sunday afternoon.

*His opening line:* "Pardon the intrusion, miss, but I couldn't help but notice you sittin' here all alone. I'd be honored to buy you a drink."

*Pros and cons:* This boy probably attended cotillion classes. He knows how to treat a lady. That said, he might not be the most progressive guy you'll ever meet—a good thing as far as chivalry goes (he'll actually go out of his way to open doors and pay the check), but not ideal when it comes to asserting your independence or your need to be right at all times.

*Future prediction:* Yours will be an elegant life of impeccable manners, country club mixers, and children who say things like "ma'am" and "please." If you're not a Southerner yourself, get ready to drink a lot of mint juleps, wear a lot of makeup, and hold your tongue (or else wage war with his conservative family) a lot of the time.

## Old-as-the-Mayflower Moneybags

*Education:* Ivy all the way. He's proud to be among the only living members of his class, and there's a branch of the library at Yale named after him.

*Occupation:* Retired. For about fifteen years.

*Never seen without:* His pacemaker.

*Real estate:* Two penthouse apartments in Manhattan, a private island in the Caribbean, and a place in Aspen. All fully staffed, in case he happens to show up.

*Fitness routine:* Since his last stroke, he's only allowed to walk around the block to get the *New York Times* every day. His butler still objects to him going alone.

*Vacation destination:* He's already seen the world. Now he just likes to get comfortable on the deck of his beach house.

*His opening line:* (Frank Sinatra song plays in the background) "I saw Ol' Blue Eyes sing at the Apollo when he was just a kid."

*Pros and cons:* Though you won't be able to take him along to your friend's twenty-fifth birthday party at Hooters, he will show you the most fabulous and romantic time when you're alone together. Much like your grandparents might, he'll make references that go right over your head and then say, "Before your time, my dear." Marrying him might seem a bit of a cliché to others, but what do you care? As long as you have separate bedrooms, go with God.

*Future prediction:* Short, so enjoy his company while he's still vertical. Expect to wear a lot of black.

## Rich Men to Avoid

When I worked in magazines, a fifty-year-old Condé Nast executive with four homes and a chauffeur once asked me to break up with his twenty-two-year-old girlfriend for him in an e-mail. This is the kind of rich guy we can do without. As Virginia Woolf put it, "On the towpath we met and had to pass a long line of imbeciles."

Sometimes the best way to know whom you want is to figure out whom you absolutely *don't* want. A rich man who doesn't treat you well, or who isn't interesting, or who loves himself more than he could ever love any woman, is quite simply not worth your time. Here are the rich men to avoid at all costs. If you meet one, run in the other direction. (Well, okay, let him buy you a drink first. But then run.)

**The rich guy who brags about his money and connections.** For a very brief time, I dated a successful New York artist who had studied at the Sorbonne, traveled the world, and sold his paintings in over forty major galleries. Yet all he ever wanted to talk about was the fact that he usually dated models (lucky me!), he owned a yacht (models always look best in their bathing suits), and he went on a bi-annual rafting trip with John Stamos. I'm sorry, but as impressive as a friendship with Uncle Jesse from *Full House* is, where's the excitement, where's the intrigue? One of the reasons that intelligent, worldly women are attracted to wealthy men, after all, is that they have the financial resources to do fascinating things. If a guy is so caught up in having money and important friends that he never uses the money for anything interesting or worthwhile, take a page from Ricki Lake, and kick him to the curb. It may seem cruel, but don't worry—there will be a gorgeous model waiting there, ready to greet him with open arms.

**The rich guy you're not really attracted to.** This one should go without saying, but drive to your local country club and check out all the pretty blondes on the arms of fat, balding men who appear to have spent more time drinking scotch in the clubhouse than hitting the course, and you'll start to wonder. I know beauty is in the eye of the beholder, but come now. Is it worth having a seven-bedroom house if you and your husband are going to need one each? This also holds true for men whom you're not attracted to mentally. If you go on a date with Boring Bob, then find yourself rushing home to call your girlfriends and gush about how great his car, watch, restaurant choice, wallet, and apartment were, but never actually mention *him,* it's time to move on. Also check your desk at work for doodles you've written absentmindedly—"[Your name] + Boring Bob's BMW Forever" should be a warning sign. Not only is this guy not worth your time, but if you're not attracted, it's unfair to him. The rich-man-dating litmus test should be as follows: always ask yourself, "Would I still be interested if he lost the money tomorrow?" If you read *Vanity Fair* (the book or the magazine) you know this is a very real possibility.

**The rich guy who's cheap.** Despite your own professional success and ambition, you've occasionally lapsed and dated the starving artist type, or the "I'm gonna start looking for a job as soon as football season ends" type, or the "What's wrong with bagging groceries if I get to keep the day-old bakery goods?" type. There's something annoying and embarrassing about the way these guys never offer to pay for anything, because quite simply, they have no money. But I believe that there is a particularly deep ring of hell reserved for the wealthy man who refuses to pay. And alas, this breed seems to be growing ever-stronger and more common due to rising confusion about who is supposed to do what on dates. I'm not saying that you should assume your boyfriend will buy you everything. I'm talking about the guy who has so much money and so little empathy that he thinks that, like him, everyone was given a little villa in Tuscany for their college graduation. The wealthy guy who expects you to be able to afford everything he can afford is not only annoying and egocentric, but also rather dumb. Next!!!

**The rich guy who tries to buy your love, forgiveness, admiration, etc.** An English friend of mine who lives in London dated a Greek shipping tycoon for nearly a year. In that time, he took her around the world, and gave her a brand-new Jaguar, an entire couture wardrobe, and a jewelry collection that rivaled the Victoria and Albert's. He also cheated on her twice, broke more dates than he kept, and was a generally sleazy guy. Their relationship ended one rainy night in his town house near Victoria Station. When he slammed the door and stormed out, she threw every last earring and silk scarf out the window at him. If she could have lifted the Jaguar, I'm sure she would have thrown that, too. What's the point of amassing presents if they're just gifts of his guilt, and they're going to end up floating in puddles eventually? You could get a second job and buy those things for yourself with all the free time you'll have now that you're not devoting precious hours to getting stood up.

**The rich guy whose friends all seem to be there for the handouts.** I first encountered this sad type in high school, when I dated a genuinely sweet kid (incidentally, the son of a millionaire) who was close friends with a posse of girls we called the LVs (because each one had a matching Louis Vuitton bag). No one ever knew quite how he fit in with them—they were snooty and vapid, while he was rather smart and dressed in ripped jeans and flannel shirts. It wasn't until I started dating him that I realized he was the LVs' benefactor. They would call him at all hours, asking to come over and swim in his pool, requesting that he pick them up in his Mercedes, and even flat-out commanding that he buy them expensive gifts (no doubt, the LVs wouldn't have been the LVs without his daddy's credit card). When I finally asked him about it, he explained that his parents had told him that the best way to make people like you is to buy them things. Yikes. Martyr that I am, I spent the next few years dating rich guys and never letting them pay for anything, as a way of showing that I liked them for them. But where's the sense in that? Trust me, when your boyfriend gets a $300 weekly allowance and you're paying for his cafeteria lunches out of your babysitting money, there's something wrong. And, like so many things in high school, this extends into your adult life. You don't want to marry into a family that teaches their children to buy people's friendship. As for Mr. LV, don't cry for him, because he's currently living in a palace in Argentina and is still surrounded by dozens of gorgeous (and no doubt, money-grubbing) women.

**The rich guy who's married or attached.** To quote Carrie Fisher in *When Harry Met Sally*, he's never going to leave his wife. The well-cared-for mistress is considered an essential belonging by a certain type of rich man, and she's not always whom you'd expect. Plenty of smart, ambitious, and otherwise sane women I know seem to think they're going to reform their married boyfriends, and can't resist all the perks of the relationship. But this sort of guy doesn't respect you, his own wife, or women in general—and if you take up with him, neither do you. No amount of affection, gifts, trips, and expensive dinners should convince you that he's worth getting to know. This guy is icky. Let him buy you a drink only if you plan to throw it in his face.

**The rich guy who will never settle down.** Most young guys, irrespective of their income brackets, practically need to be shot with a tranquilizer gun before they agree to walk down the aisle. But as they get older, many men realize that the companionship, stability, and love they're gaining through commitment are worth giving up partying, playing air-guitar in their underwear, and the chance to act on things if Heidi Klum should ever take a wrong turn and end up in their driveway. Some less-evolved men, however, never quite get it. And a lot of them are rich. Why? Because they can. For some women, money covers a multitude of sins (see all of the above), including fear of commitment. Don't be one of them. Remember the rich guy litmus test: would you tolerate his inability to settle down if he didn't have the money? Enough said.

**The rich guy who rests on his rich guy laurels.** My friend was once at a society ball in Houston, when a not-so-handsome man came up to her and said, "Hi, I'm Phil. I'm extremely rich and I'd like to take you to dinner." Apparently, Phil did not believe in beating around the bush. Against her better judgment, my friend agreed to go. It turned out that he had told her everything she needed to know in that first interaction—his name was indeed Phil, he was indeed extremely rich, and he did indeed want to take her to dinner. Unfortunately, beyond that he had no interests, no redeeming qualities, and nothing interesting to say. Any guy who identifies himself as rich, or tells you how much he makes on a first encounter (or a second, third, or fourth encounter for that matter), isn't worth your time.

## Assessing What He's Worth

An important thing to remember about dating wealthy men is that rich means different things to different people. You might want to marry a man with enough money to send your kids to college, or you might want to marry a man with enough money to start a college of his own on one of his nine private islands. Each of these desires will have to be satisfied in a different way. Location factors in as well. Those of us in New York City need look no farther than Wall Street if we want to find a man with money. But how do you know where to look if there isn't an entire section of your city or town where all the wealthiest men congregate?

According to the Occupational Employment and Wage Estimates provided by the Department of Labor's Bureau of Labor Statistics (BLS), the top twenty highest-paying professions in the United States and their mean average salaries are as follows. (As you'll see, a good place to find a new favorite coffee shop or get lost and ask for directions is right next door to your local hospital. And thankfully, we've all got one of those.)

- Surgeons: $190,280
- Anesthesiologists: $184,880
- Obstetricians and gynecologists: $180,660
- Internists, general: $160,130
- Pediatricians, general: $143,300
- Chief executives: $140,580
- Family and general practitioners: $139,640
- Psychiatrists: $139,300
- Dentists: $131,210

- Airline pilots, copilots, and flight engineers: $129,880
- Lawyers: $107,800
- Podiatrists: $106,430
- Engineering managers: $99,710
- Computer and information systems managers: $95,230
- Optometrists: $95,060
- Natural sciences managers: $93,990
- Air traffic controllers: $93,240
- Marketing managers: $92,190
- Sales managers: $91,840
- Law teachers, postsecondary: $91,420

## Top Ten Places to Meet a Quality Man

Now that you have a sense of the quality men who are out there (and how much money they make), the next step is to find one. After surveying the social habits of great guys and the women who marry them, I came up with the following list of places to look.

1. **The gym.** Okay, this might seem counterintuitive—people are always saying you can meet guys at the gym, but in the end it just sounds ridiculous to you. After all,

when you're there, you're sweating, your face gets red and splotchy, and you just want to focus on surviving another fifteen minutes on the treadmill. But what I'm suggesting is that you treat the gym like you would a singles bar. This is better for your social life *and* your wallet. Run or walk outdoors for exercise, or join a cheap gym in your neighborhood. Then, once or twice a month, go to an upscale gym that's full of rich men. Wear your cutest workout clothes, make a lot of eye contact, and ask the nearest hottie in a Yale Law T-shirt for help on your form.

Most upscale gyms have day rates. Crunch Fitness charges $24 a day to nonmembers. Asphalt Green in New York City is a five-and-a-half-acre workout palace with an Olympic-size swimming pool and touch football games (read: men who went to prep school) and it also offers day rates. Another option in New York, Chicago, and Los Angeles is the Fitness Access Passbook, a plan sponsored by The American Health and Fitness Alliance. You pay $75 for a passbook (it's good for one year) and get access to almost every gym in the city (two to five visits per location plus four personal training sessions). If you spot a cute guy and want to join his gym for real, your $75 fee is usually deducted from the membership cost. There's even a passbook just for yoga studios, if you like your men flexible.

2. **Ivy League clubs.** Every Ivy League university has clubs in most major cities. The Harvard Club in New York includes a restaurant, bar, spa, gym, swimming pool, and

## How to Order a Drink

What a man drinks (and how he orders it) speaks volumes about him. And the same goes for you. Avoid ordering fruity, trendy drinks (basically anything neon pink or green that comes in a martini glass) when you're in the company of men. Stick to the classics—gin or vodka martinis, gin and tonics, or just a glass of white wine; show that you're sophisticated and have a timeless sense of style. Here are some other tips and terms for impressing the guy beside you at the bar.

- **Order top-shelf liquor only:** Tanqueray No. Ten, Bombay Sapphire, Johnny Walker Black, etc. The extra couple of bucks you'll spend will be worth their weight in gold (or diamonds) when they get you noticed by a successful man.
- **"On the rocks":** means with ice.
- **"Neat":** means leave it alone, don't add any mixer.
- **"Dirty":** means with a bit of olive brine added.
- **"Splash":** means a few drops.
- **"Tipping":** means 20 percent per drink, no matter what. If you have a tab open, it's okay to wait until the end of the night to tip, but otherwise you should do it with each drink. (Don't worry, there won't be too many. I have a rule that I always buy my own first drink. This gives me a little time to get a feel for the crowd and decide who I want to buy me my second.)

squash courts. So whatever it is you like to do—be it eating out or working out—you can most likely do it there, in the company of well-educated men. If you went to an Ivy, you're in luck. If not, don't worry—any friend with an Ivy League degree can bring you along as a guest. Meeting men at the Ivy clubs is one of the best weeding-out techniques I've ever seen. You know where he went to school within a matter of seconds. If he has an account at the bar (no money is exchanged at an Ivy club), then he's legit. If not, he's probably just a hanger-on.

3. **Bars.** A little bit of research can help you figure out which bars are packed full of successful men. Generally, you will have good luck at any bar in close proximity to your city's financial district, particularly between the hours of 6:30 and 11:00 on Monday through Thursday nights. Bankers flock there after a hard day's work. If you can get there in time for happy hour, position yourself near the bar so you can get a good look at the men who come in (and at what they're ordering). A word of caution from my friend James, a Wall Street trader: according to him, the majority of women in these places are decked out in full makeup and tube tops on a Tuesday evening. "You can tell they're only there to meet guys, and they obviously are not coming from work," James says. "They're the kind of girls you take home, but not the kind of girls you'd take home to Mom." Use caution. Wear your work clothes. And leave the blue eye shadow at home.

4. **Volunteering.** As discussed in chapter 1, rich men do a lot of volunteer work. Meeting a guy this way is ideal be-

cause it shows you that he has an interest in improving the world, and sends him the same message about you. Also, his mother will love you based solely on the way you met.

5. **On the field.** Every girl I know who has joined a co-ed sports team has met a guy doing it. Stick with the prep school sports if you want to ensure that a good number of available cultured men will be there. Soccer, sailing, skiing, running, tennis, lacrosse, and squash are particularly fruitful.

6. **Charity/political fund-raisers.** You know what they say about shooting fish in a barrel. Since these can be extremely pricey events, it's best to attend as someone's guest. This is the time to put all you've learned about how to interact with cultured people into play. Mingle, meet many men, and don't drink too much. Cozying up to older women might prove helpful—mothers and grandmothers are always on the lookout for their sons and grandsons.

7. **Jazz bars.** Quite a separate category from bars in general. There is something in the DNA of all rich men that makes them like jazz. This is particularly true of the older set. For example, one Saturday night I was on a date at my favorite place in Manhattan—Bemelmans Bar at the Carlyle Hotel. When my date excused himself to go to the restroom, I was approached by Harry, a fifty-something oil mogul in town from Texas. He asked if I'd like to have dinner with him the following night,

and I said no. He then lifted his hand to shake mine and pressed a key into my palm. "It's for my suite at the Plaza," he said. "I only use it once a month, so it's all yours if you want it." I never did go to the suite, nor do I think Harry was marriage material, but all the same, it has to be said—rich men and jazz go together like a wink and a smile.

8. **Department stores.** A good friend of mine met her fiancé while shopping for a sweater for her brother at Barneys. She spotted a gorgeous guy in Armani (turns out he's a millionaire) and delivered the classic line: "You're about my brother's size—would you mind trying this on?" The men's department of any major store is full of dating prospects, and since there are a lot fewer women there than in a bar or club, you'll get their undivided attention.

9. **On an airplane.** Every time you fly, try as hard as you can to upgrade your ticket to First Class. There you will find an array of executives with hours of free time on their hands.

10. **In the mail/online.** Don't have time to join a team or troll the Ivy League clubs? Working girl, meet your new best friend. The Social Register is a directory of people who make up the most elite portion of society in a given city. (They're available in New York, Washington, D.C., Philadelphia, Chicago, Boston, St. Louis, Pittsburgh, Cleveland, Cincinnati, Dayton, San Francisco, Baltimore, and Buffalo.) It lists rich men by name, address of

first and second home, college attended (and what year they graduated), and marital status. Think of it like a map of the stars' homes in Hollywood—use it to pinpoint the areas where you should be grocery shopping, taking your dry cleaning, and eating out. To obtain a copy, write to The Social Register Association, 381 Park Avenue South, New York, NY 10016.

If it's a banker you're after, you can also check out the magazine *Trader Monthly.* They run a feature called "Trader Dater"—sort of like a personal ad section exclusively for bankers and the women who wish to date them. And if you'd like to find a well-educated man while sitting at home in your footie pajamas, go to www.rightstuffdating.com. It's a site only for people who have attended the most exclusive colleges and universities in the country, so you can rest assured that while you're meeting a guy who gets dates online, he did not get his degree there.

## The Fine Art of Flirting

Now that you know where to find the best men, it's time to think about how you'll act once you do. Remember my friend James's distinction—there are girls you take home, and girls you take home to Mom. If it's marriage you're after, there are a few basic rules for how to act when you meet a quality man. Follow them, and I promise he will call.

**Learn to flirt.** For weeks I had been hearing about this woman named Shelby, a magazine editor who had just moved to Manhattan from Savannah, Georgia. "She's so great," my friend Amanda told me. "We went out on Tuesday and met six different guys. She's like a man magnet." "I did her hair and she talked about the new hotshot attorney she's seeing," my friend Clint, a stylist at Vidal Sassoon, gushed. "She's such a riot!" Even a couple of my straight male friends talked about her—they'd met her at a book party, and each one begged me to set him up, figuring that since I used to work in magazines, I must have some "in" with her.

A few days later, I finally got to meet Shelby for myself. My first thought was something along the lines of "What the hell was all that fuss about?" Shelby is five-four, maybe 140 pounds, with shoulder-length brown hair and a pretty smile. A cute girl, but nothing to write home about. However, once we started talking, I understood. Shelby is enchanting because she's always engaged, always listening. She'll lightly touch your arm, she'll meet your eye as you talk to her, and she'll never look over your shoulder to see who else is in the room.

Spend time observing singles in any social setting, and you'll see that the women who catch men's attention are not always the prettiest or the best-dressed. They are the ones who know how to flirt. Flirting is about give and take. Ask him questions and genuinely listen to his answers (don't just think about what you should say next). Touch him gently now and then, and never look away from him while you're talking. Being flirty has nothing to do with romance, and everything to do with making another person feel good about him- or herself. It is an attitude that you can learn by practicing on people in whom you have no romantic interest whatsoever—smile warmly at the woman on the treadmill beside you at the gym, be extra thankful to the kid behind the counter at the grocery store, compliment your boss on her new perfume. So many women think that the best way to get a man is to act cool and removed. These are the same women who later complain that their boyfriends don't listen or care how they feel.

Kindness begets kindness. The reason why straight women, gay men, and former fratboys alike all love Shelby is because she's kind and listens to them with interest. She makes them each feel special. She knows how to flirt. I asked her to help me devise some guidelines for flawless flirting, and here's what we came up with.

**Make eye contact.** The first exchange you share with a potential mate will not be verbal or physical. It's all in the eyes. If you catch his eye from across a crowded room, smile and make contact, but look away after three seconds. Don't stare, or keep looking over your shoulder. Just a brief glance and a real connection should be enough to draw him to you if he's interested.

**Be aware of your body language.** I recently learned that Oxford University has an entire center devoted to the science of flirting. Why have they not yet recruited me to work there? Your guess is as good as mine. The central premise of their flirtation method has to do with body language. Here's what they say: "When you first approach an attractive stranger, having established at least an indication of mutual interest through eye contact, try to make eye contact again at about four feet away, before moving any closer. At four feet (about two small steps away), you are on the borderline between what are known as the 'social zone' (four to twelve feet) and the 'personal zone' (eighteen inches to four feet). If you receive a positive response at four feet, move in to 'arm's length' (about two feet, six inches). If you try to approach much closer than this, particularly if you try to cross the eighteen-inch personal zone/intimate zone border, your target may feel uncomfortable. The 'intimate zone' (less than eighteen inches) is reserved for lovers, family, and very close friends. If you are close enough to whisper and be heard, you are probably too close for comfort." Of course, they're British, so take that with a grain of salt. But I tested the theory, as any good scientist would, and it actually works.

**Play Oprah.** I'm not saying that you should fawn all over a new guy, but every man loves to talk about himself. Again, ask him lots of questions, and take cues—if he seems particularly interested in talking about his recent vacation in Morocco, don't change the subject to your upcoming trip to Aspen just yet. Instead, ask him about what he saw, ate, did and so on. Almost everyone asks the same questions of strangers in bars or at parties: where did you go to school, and what do you do? We ask these questions for good reason—they provide us with landmarks for figuring out whom we're talking to. However, if you want to set yourself apart and seem more interesting, ask original, open-ended questions. (He's bound to get around to telling you what he does at some point.)

**Know your audience.** To illustrate this very important point, let me tell you a little story about a man I like to call Pitcher Perfect. I met him at a party in Boston, and he was just coming up to play major-league baseball after two years on a farm team. He was gorgeous. He was funny. He loved kids. He was about to start making a million dollars a year to run around throwing a ball in tight white pants. We had a nice chat for an hour or so, and when the conversation turned to the great American pastime, I chose to tell a story about how my sister and I had been present for one of the biggest Red Sox victories of all time, and that as it occurred we were discussing her latest crush in the stands and had no idea that something monumentous had happened until the crowd started screaming. I'd always thought the story was funny, but when he excused himself from the conversation a moment later, I realized that perhaps I'd chosen the wrong crowd to tell it to. It's important to be yourself from the beginning, but remember that men are extremely insecure creatures. They need to feel impressive in order to feel attractive.

**Don't dress too provocatively.** What were you wearing when you met your last serious boyfriend? I was wrapped up in a winter coat, gloves, and a scarf. I asked a bunch of my girlfriends this same question, and the vast majority of them were not dressed like a window display at Frederick's of Hollywood either. In fact, most of them were in work clothes, jeans, or formalwear. A first impression is instantaneous, but extremely powerful. If you look pretty, but also leave a little bit (or a lot) to the imagination, you will attract the right kind of man.

If a guy sees you in a halter top, miniskirt, and stilettos, he will be picturing you in a Budweiser ad, not at a family dinner.

**Laugh.** It's easier for some of us to be natural and comfortable around new people than it is for others, but remember: all this flirtation is supposed to be fun. If you find yourself in a conversation with a new man, and you are not legitimately laughing and enjoying yourself, take stock of the situation. Is it because you are too shy and self-conscious? If so, what can you do to feel more confident next time? (See page 131 for some suggestions.) If it's just that this particular man doesn't do it for you, excuse yourself from the conversation and find someone else with whom to talk.

**Resist the urge to keep talking.** Refrain from chatting until the bar lights go up, or the gym lights go down. Despite what I've told you about being kind, acting interested in his opinions, and asking questions that show you want to know more about him, the most crucial step in the flirting process is knowing when, and how, to walk away. So many women I know gush about a guy they've just met, and how they talked all night long, only to never hear from the guy again. Most men like a challenge. When you feel that you've almost reached the height of your conversation, excuse yourself to go check on a friend.

**Don't touch him too much.** At most, lightly brush his arm when you walk away. Leave him wanting more and he's guaranteed to come and get it. My friends and I call this *breeziness.* It is a well-documented fact that no man (or woman, for that matter) can resist breeziness. As soon as you appear slightly unattainable, that guy will want to attain you. When he tracks you down and asks for your number, give it to him with a smile, tell him it was great meeting him, and excuse yourself again.

## SECRET WEAPON: Making Flirtation Fun Again

While interviewing women and men for this book, I kept hearing the same complaints about meeting new people: it's too much work, it gets monotonous, it's hard to think of things to talk about besides "What do you do?" and "Where are you from?" With all of this negativity surrounding flirtation, it's a wonder that anyone gets off the couch on Saturday night. Flirting can be lots of fun. Though you're looking to meet and settle down with a quality man, that doesn't mean you can't laugh yourself silly in the process. Most flirtation is ultimately fruitless, but flirting is a skill, and like any skill, it improves only with practice. If you don't meet someone worthwhile the first time or even the second, keep it up. I guarantee you'll find yourself out on a date with a great guy in the very near future. And if sweatpants are starting to look more appealing than Jimmy Choos, grab a bunch of girlfriends and revive your flirt quotient at a bar or party with one or more of the following tricks. Yes, they're goofy, but I actually know women who have met their husbands while playing these games. Why? Because when you're enjoying yourself, it shows, and men are all the more drawn to you.

**Offbeat conversations.** When you find yourself nodding off into your vodka-tonic while talking to a nice new guy, infuse the conversation with (light!) unusual topics. Ask him what song is his personal anthem, the no-longer-in-existence band he'd choose to see in concert, or which historical figure he'd most like to make out with. This tactic is a little bit stale, but it can be amusing, and lead to a stand-out conversation that allows you to come across as memorable without divulging a lot of personal information.

**The best pick-up line ever used.** For a while, the Manhattan singles scene was so bleak that it even turned me off. The same predictable crowd night after night, the same lame guys with the same lame pick-up lines. Why is it that only a certain type of guy (the type you don't want to meet) uses pick-up lines, while other, more quality men tend to talk among themselves? Whatever the case, I decided to turn the tables. Each time I walked into a bar, I'd stake out the best-looking man in a Polo shirt, tap him on the shoulder, and say, "Excuse me, what's your name?" When he told me, I'd smile and say, "Great, thanks. I just thought I should know the name of the cutest guy in this bar." Cheesy, but it worked! I got several free drinks and went on a few great dates, all thanks to that ridiculous line. Men aren't used to being complimented in such an outright way, so a lot of them find it flattering. Just remember that after you make the initial bold move, you should slide right back into the role of the person being wooed. You paid him a compliment, but that doesn't mean that you should buy him a drink or ask him out.

**Accents and props.** A group of extremely attractive banker guys I know in Boston swear by prop flirting. They go out every weekend and use a different theme to attract women. Sometimes they wear capes, sometimes they wear eye patches, once they wore chicken suits. Again, goofy, but doesn't just picturing it make you smile? Including props (and accents if you can pull them off) into your flirtation routine will help you stand out from the sea of women in black camisoles and halters, and show that you don't take yourself all that seriously. It's about letting your guard down, so that a new man will do the same. Six months ago, the Boston bankers had a party at their loft. When guests arrived, they were handed a bowl of fake mustaches and told that they had to wear one if they wanted to come inside. Several successful couples formed that night. If you can flirt with someone while you're both doing your best Groucho impressions, then you can easily find plenty to talk about for months to come (and if you stay together, you'll have a fantastic meeting story).

**Competitions.** Double-standard alert! If I heard about the following from a bunch of former frat boys, I would most likely rail on for hours about how disgusting men are. But oh well. When I was in college, each year the girls in my dorm held a Man Competition. I always won, hands down. One year, we competed to see who could get dates with one guy from each Ivy League school the fastest. Another year, it was who could date guys from the most foreign countries in six months. Competing with friends over dating might give you the heebie-jeebies, but it's a good tool to utilize because it sharpens your flirting skills and helps you remember that until you find someone worthwhile, dating is just a game. Too many of us meet a new guy and fixate on him before we even know his middle name. It's important to avoid this trap and date a lot of men (plus, it's fun to say that you won the Man Competition four years running).

## Flirting in Different Settings

All of the rules and tips mentioned so far are important for when you're meeting men at parties, bars, or other social events. But the majority of us meet in less obvious settings. Here's how to navigate flirtations in some of the most common locations:

**At work.** Official comment on office romance: it's not a good idea. If things don't work out, you'll still have to see each other at staff meetings and by the coffee machine every morning. For a while, I dated a guy who worked on another floor in my building. To this day, when I see him in the cafeteria, I have to fight the urge to hide behind the salad bar. Unofficially though, the office can be a great place to meet men—most of us spend the vast majority of our time there, so it's only natural that office romances occur. And men from work come prescreened: you know what they do, a bit about who they are, and how they interact with others on a day-to-day basis. The main rule of office flirtation is to be incredibly slow and covert. This is not the time to go balls to the wall and ask a guy out because he smiled at you last Tuesday. Let him do all the wooing. Flirt through glances, smiles, and brief in-person chats. Do not send him flirtatious e-mails via your work account, don't gossip about your coworkers together as a way of getting close, and resist the urge to tell your eight closest office friends all the details.

**At school.** Several of my friends recently left their jobs to start law or medical school. And without exception, the first thing they reported on (before classes or housing or grades) was the fresh crop of men in their lives. Beware: law school and medical school are forays into the professional world. They are not College Part Deux. The men you meet there will likely be your colleagues for years to come, so use the same discretion that you would in an office romance. One of the great benefits of meeting someone in this environment (or at work) is that you are more likely to be up front with and kind to one another. Remember that most relationships end, and you want your reputation to remain pristine if this happens to be one of them.

**Online.** In the past few years, online romance has gone from slightly suspect and weird to entirely acceptable and common. The success that friends of mine have had on J-Date alone makes me wish that I were one of the Chosen People. Online dating is a unique situation, with a set of flirtation rules all its own. First off, your profile: be honest with potential matches. Don't use a picture that looks nothing like you, don't say you love skydiving or Quentin Tarantino movies unless it's the truth. For some reason, online love tends to lead to a lot of little white lies. Perhaps because it starts out as very anonymous, or perhaps because everyone is trying to look more desirable than the competition. Whatever the case, don't begin a relationship—even if it's just one date—in a deceitful way. Once you've made a connection with someone, it's smartest to meet him (in a very public place!) after just two or three brief conversations, rather than talking for hours and hours, for weeks on end. Why? Because of a dating danger my friends and I call *Dirty Socks vs. Two Souls Floating.* The best relationship is one in which you and your mate agree on and can discuss theoretical issues like politics and philosophy, but also watch hours of *Best Week Ever* together in your sweatpants. In other words, it's important to know that you could exist as two souls floating, just all ideas and feelings, *and* that you can deal with his dirty socks piled on the floor. When you meet someone online, he exists only as a theoretical (two souls floating) until the moment you meet face-to-face. He may share your beliefs about Kant, but if you can't stand watching him chew or the way he addresses a waitress, you won't be able to coexist in the real world for long (dirty socks). One last word on online flirtation: remember that each time you put something in print and click "Send," you are in danger of having your words broadcast to the universe, so use discretion.

## Waiting for Him to Call

I have always assumed that when Tom Petty wrote "The waiting is the hardest part," he was three days into the agonizing process of "Well, is she going to call, or isn't she?" There are few things in life more maddening. But, as this book will tell you again and again, the secret to happy, healthy relationships can be summed up in just one word: patience. After you meet a new man, he has a full week to call you before you should:

a. Freak out.

b. Write him off.

Whenever they are waiting for that first call, women I know (myself very much included) tend to worry about the upcoming weekend. If he waits until Thursday, can they still accept weekend plans? If he calls during the workday on Friday, should they call him back right away or wait until Monday? Forget about the upcoming weekend. If he's worth seeing, you can get together *next* weekend, or the following. The now-or-never approach to meeting someone is a surefire way to end up in a drunk-dialing dilemma, or some equally embarrassing act.

He's either going to call or he isn't. The amount of time he takes to do so depends on his schedule, his self-esteem, and how many times he's seen *Swingers.* It is doubtful that it has anything to do with how much he likes you. If he hasn't called you after seven days, it's safe to assume that you are not a priority. So forget about him then, and if he calls later, tell him you're much too busy to see him. But, in the meantime, here's how to stay sane between the moment you hand him your number and the moment the phone rings.

**Erase his number.** If you meet someone and he asks for your number, chances are he will give you his as well. Don't refuse it, but as soon as you are out of his presence, erase it from your phone, or rip up his card. Make sure that there is no way for you to get in touch with him. Making the first call is his job. Don't allow your eagerness to know how things are going to play out let you forget it.

**Make plans for the following weekend.** One way to avoid all that "Will he call in time for the weekend?" stress is to ensure that, either way, you will be fully booked. There is nothing more embarrassing and sad than leaving your entire calendar open for someone with whom you have not made plans. Telling him that you're busy makes you look more desirable anyway.

**Give yourself a cut-off time.** There's no reason to start hyperventilating about when he's going to call six hours after you meet. So give yourself a day (I'd suggest day three) at which point you are allowed to start worrying. Then, for those first few days, just push him from your thoughts. Murphy's Law says that the second you stop thinking of him, the phone will ring.

**Leave your phone at home.** If you can part with it for the entire day, leave your phone at home while you're at work or out with friends. That way, you avoid having to deal with the urge to check it every forty-five seconds to see whether or not he's called.

**Keep meeting people.** Too many women fall into the trap of thinking there is only one great guy out there for them—and he usually tends to be the last guy they've met. Just because you hit it off with the Dartmouth alum beside you on the red-eye to LA does not mean that the two of you are now promised to one another. The more men you meet, the less undue emphasis you will place on any one of them.

**If he calls at a strange time . . .** When my friend April started dating her long-term boyfriend Patrick, she complained that he only ever called her on her cell phone, when he knew she'd be at work. We surmised that he did this because he was nervous about actually speaking to her. Ultimately, Patrick confirmed our suspicions (like a lot of men, he's a total phone-phobe), and eventually he started calling April at night. No big deal. Sometimes these things just take a little time to sort themselves out. That said, I don't know a single married woman whose success story begins with, "Well, we met at the gym on a Wednesday, he asked me for my number, and then he called on Saturday at two in the morning." The guy who calls you in the middle of the night is transparent, rude, and going nowhere. Do not call him back, no matter what.

## Asking Him Out: How to Know if You Should Take the Plunge

Is it ever okay for a woman to ask a man out? Not since the whole flat-earth/round-earth thing have great minds disagreed so often and so passionately on a subject. The best scenario is the one in which he asks you out. Men like a challenge, and it's good (at least for the first few dates) to keep them guessing. If you're in a bar or party scenario where you've just met a guy you like, followed the rules of flirting, and he hasn't asked for your number, *move on.* But it's okay to ask him out if you know him semi-well (or very well) and:

- **You have it on good authority that he likes you.** Some guys are chronically shy. If you've had your eye on a man in your social circle, and everyone keeps talking about how much he wants to ask you out, it's okay to give him a little nudge. While you're out as a group, take him aside and suggest that the two of you grab drinks sometime. Let him know he should call you to arrange it. This should give him enough guts to seal the deal.

- **You know that he's clueless.** The type of guy who is charming, but doesn't have an ounce of game or any sense of how to pursue a woman, can seem childish and annoying—but he can also make a great and honest boyfriend once you've shown him a thing or two. Again, give him a nudge. Say it would be great to have a drink sometime (don't specify when) and let him propose a location and night. This allows him to maintain a bit of traditional manliness, and helps you swallow the knowledge that you made the first move.

- **You know there's a reason he hasn't asked you yet.** Sorry, but the reason can't be because he already has a girlfriend or because he doesn't like you. What I mean by this one is that romance is complicated and there's a lot of gray area. Maybe he asked you out two years ago during your punk rocker phase and you turned him down, but his Brooks Brothers suits have become more appealing in your old age. Maybe you used to have a crush on his friend (the punk rocker, perhaps?), and he knows it. Whatever. Use your instinct. Ask a man out only if you know he will be delighted, and that he would have asked you out first if not for extenuating circumstances. But after you make the first (subtle) gesture, leave the rest of the wooing up to him.

## Remember Why You're Out There in the First Place

My first year of high school, I fell hopelessly in love with a boy who was hopelessly in love with the heavy metal band Metallica. I'm ashamed to say that I went right out and bought every one of their albums, played them at top volume on my Discman whenever he was nearby, and even orchestrated a humiliating scene at our local skating rink, in which I just happened to be sitting in the bleachers reading my favorite book—*Metallica: Ride the Lightning*—when he came off the ice. I still think one should be open to a man's interests, but there's a difference between being open to them, and lying to the poor guy (and to your poor self) about how you feel. I loathed Metallica. And I'm sure you won't be shocked to hear that it didn't work out between me and Metal Boy. I tried to mold myself into exactly the girl he was looking for, and that doesn't work. Besides which, it isn't any fun.

High school is over, but I know several women who are still playing the Metallica game in new relationships. When you're meeting men, it's important to ask questions and be attentive. But it's even more important to remember the tried-and-oh-so-true cliché: there are other fish in the sea. You should never alter yourself in any way for the sake of some guy you've known for five minutes. Too many women get stuck in the trap of trying to snag one particular man. If he's not pursuing you from the get-go, drop him like a hot potato. There's more where he came from.

# The First Date

"The only thing that went down with any regularity on Charlotte's dates was a gold American Express card."

—*Sex and the City*

Congratulations! You've passed the first hurdles. You've found a successful guy and you've gotten him to call you. This is no small feat. The first date is the next step, and it's a crucial one. The same rules apply as on the night you met—don't divulge too much personal information, ask him a lot of (not-too-probing) questions about his interests and experiences, and leave him wanting more in every possible way (you know what I'm talking about).

This chapter will help you navigate the night of nights, but first, remember this: a very wise couples therapist I know says that a man will tell you everything you need to know about him on a first date, so it's up to you to hear him. Case in point: my friend Jill met a fantastic young architect at a party. They hit it off and decided to meet for drinks later that week. Over drinks he said casually (well, as casually as one can say something like this) that his parents had gone through a truly heinous divorce, and he knew that he would never get married. Jill mentioned it to her twelve closest friends, and every one of us said not to worry about it—it was only a first date, after all. And plenty of guys think they'll never get married, but those guys had never met her. Three years later, they were still together, and she was itching for a ring. She hinted. She sighed and lingered at the window each time they walked by Tiffany's. Finally, she flipped, and screamed, "When are you going to propose?!" His answer: "I'm not getting married. I told you that on our first date."

Not that people can't change their minds—it happens all the time. But way too many women fall into the trap of taking a man's admitted shortcomings as a personal challenge, rather than a warning sign. If he says he doesn't get along with his parents, don't picture yourself as Ali McGraw in *Love Story*, reuniting them in a tearful, well-orchestrated meeting. Instead, consider what that means to you. Do you care if the man you're with isn't close to his family? Take what he says at face value. Don't infer or create your own back-story. If he says he's not looking for something serious, chances are, he's not looking for something serious. Why make it your job to convince him otherwise? You don't have that kind of free time.

## Google-Stalking 101

A first date is like a job interview, and the more information you have about your interviewer beforehand, the better. I will never forget a classmate of mine who coasted through high school with a C average at best, but still assured everyone that she was going to Stanford. On the day she got her acceptance letter, we were all stunned. I asked her how she'd done it. Secret family connections she hadn't mentioned before? A pact with the Devil, perhaps?

Nope, she told me. It was just good, old-fashioned research. Apparently, she did a little detective work before her interview and found out that the man who would determine her fate at Stanford had written two books of poetry. She may have been a C-student, but this chick was clever. She tracked down the books (both out of print), read and memorized them, and then feigned surprise and awe upon meeting the creator of her two all-time favorite volumes of poetry at the interview.

Not that I'm advocating lying on your first date. I'm just saying it's best to gather as much information as you can ahead of time. The Girl Scout motto isn't "Be prepared" for nothing. So what are the best ways to get information? Clearly, any single girl this side of Amish country knows to Google her potential boyfriends, but I am astounded at how sloppy some women are with their Googling. It's not just as simple as typing a guy's name into the blank box and hitting "Search." Karin, one of my very best friends, taught me the real way to Google-stalk. I'd call her and tell her that some man I'd just met was un-Googleable, she'd ask me for his name, and thirty seconds later, just by pressing a few extra buttons, she'd bring up twenty sites listing his full title and contact information at work, all the awards he'd won in college, his high school basketball stats, any volunteer organizations he was a part of, a satellite photo of his house (seriously) and a composite of what our future children would look like (not seriously, but wouldn't that be cool?).

I asked Karin to help me compile the following cheat sheet to Extreme-Googling, but before you read it, one warning—make sure that once you're on the date, you *never let on that you've Googled him to within an inch of his life!* Use information you've gathered about him to lead the conversation, rather than lead him to seek a restraining order against you. A friend of mine was out on a first date with a young Washington speechwriter, and things were going great. After finishing one bottle of wine and moving on to their second, he started to tell her a story about how he'd almost won a national spelling bee in eighth grade, but had lost to his own cousin. Unfortunately, he'd told the same story to his college paper and my friend had read it online, so when he got to the punch line and said, "Guess which word I got out on?" my friend busted out, "Familial!" and started laughing. The speechwriter wasn't so amused by his psychic companion. That relationship ended in the first round. O-V-E-R. Over.

Let's start with the basics. At the very least, it's imperative to do both a Google search and a Yahoo! search (each can yield different results) and follow these steps.

1. Enter your man's name in quotations. For example, if you're searching for Peter Smith, enter "Peter Smith" into the search box. This way the search engine knows

to look for only the full name, not all instances of Peter or Smith.

2. Doing just a first and last name search (always in quotes!) can give you way too many results in some cases, or not enough in others. Try variations on his name, such as "Pete Smith." A middle name or initial can also be helpful in finding results, especially if his name is common.

3. Once you've done a basic name search, do some other Google and Yahoo! searches using any information you have about him (e.g., his name paired with his hometown, the college he attended, the company he works for). For some reason, entering "Peter Smith, Cornell University," or "Peter Smith, Chicago, IL" can bring up results that a basic name search can't.

4. If he's registered with them, Web sites like Friendster and MySpace are great for getting straight-from-the-source information about his interests, hobbies, and friends.

5. Try looking on his company's Web site and searching for him by name. Large companies will often have a listing of employee information, with full titles, contact information, and photos. If he's an attorney, you're in luck, because every lawyer in the United States has a bio (and sometimes a photograph, suitable for forwarding on to friends) on www.martindale.com.

6. Gone are the days of asking where he lives and then driving by with binoculars to take a look. The modern

dater (or stalker, whichever you prefer) needs only a laptop and a Web address—www.zabasearch.com will show you an actual picture of your man's house, and the only information you'll need to get it is his full name and home state.

7. If you're really obsessive, you might find it useful to get information on his hometown, or the town where he currently lives. Log on to www.city-data.com to find the median income and house price, the education level of the town's population, crime rates, marriage statistics, and data on how the town stacks up against others in the same state.

## Before You Go

Now that you're armed with information about your date, it's time to think about actually going out with him. The rules of flirting from chapter 2 still apply: ask him a lot about himself, know your audience, dress appropriately (i.e., covered enough so that if you ran into your grandmother, she wouldn't have a stroke), and don't divulge too much personal information. I can't stress it enough—treat these early encounters like a job interview. By that, I don't mean that you need to sell yourself to this guy, or tell him if you were a tree what kind of a tree you would be, and why. I just mean that you should be discreet, and try to figure out not only if you're right for him, but if he's right for you. When you apply for a job, you want to put your best self forward, but you also want to know what you're getting into. There are plenty of jobs that you could get in a heartbeat that are completely beneath you. And so it is with men. A first date is not a relationship, just like interviewing for a job is nothing like actually doing the job. In both cases, it's a chance to get a little more information so you can make an informed decision about how to proceed.

### SECRET WEAPON: I Have Confidence in Me

It's normal to feel a little nervous before a first date. And by "a little nervous" I mean queasy, nauseous, light-headed, self-conscious, and a candidate for worst-dressed lists everywhere, even if you picked the perfect outfit the night before. Just remember that he's going out with you for a reason. And if that fails, go with these hokey, yet tried-and-true confidence boosters.

**Think of the hardest thing you've ever done.** When I was in third grade and had stage fright before a ballet recital, my best friend's mother whispered to me, "You can do it. And after you do, you'll always remember that if you can do this, you can do anything." Now granted, I've done tougher things by this point in my life than "Shuffle Off to Buffalo" with a bunch of eight-year-olds, but when I'm up against a task that seems too daunting to take on, I still always remember that I got out there and danced my little heart out, even when I thought I couldn't. So before you start breathing into a paper bag over a silly date, try to recall the scariest thing you ever thought you couldn't do, but did. Maybe it was landing a great job, or closing a killer deal, or just wearing a tutu in front of fifty people. Whatever the case, you did it. You can certainly handle a dinner out with a new man.

**Pretend you're someone else.** Not to contradict that last tip, but sometimes an extra burst of confidence comes from playing a part. When I'm feeling a little bit fat, for instance, I always pretend I'm Cindy Crawford. Ain't no one calling Cindy fat. Silly, but it actually works. Likewise, when you're feeling nervous about a date, it can help to channel the most secure, self-assured person you know. It might be Carrie Bradshaw, or your second cousin Wendy, or the annoyingly lucky cheerleader you hated (and envied) in high school. Whoever. Just pretend you're her as you greet your date, and you'll feel cool, calm, and collected.

**Call on your fan club.** We all have people in our lives who think we're simply the greatest. Before a first date, get your biggest fan on the phone—be it a friend, a sister, or your mom—and explain that you need a little reminder of how fabulous you are. She will be more than happy to let you know.

## Choosing Your First Date Spot

People put too much emphasis on the location of a first date. *We went hang-gliding!* makes for an interesting story, but how much can you learn about a person when you're flying through the air together? Likewise, who are all these people going to the movies on a first date? Unless you're whispering, "So, how many siblings do you have?" during the love scenes, how can you learn anything about a person from sitting in a darkened theater with him?

The ideal first date is dinner out. (You can go hang-gliding afterward if you must.) Choose a restaurant where you will be comfortable. If there's a place in your neighborhood that you love, go there. If you're not the most adventurous of eaters, don't try to impress your date with the newest Japanese-Cajun fusion bistro in town. But if food is your thing, by all means, show him what you've got. Of course, chances are he will suggest someplace. Go along with it if it appeals to you, but if not, speak up. Once a guy wanted to take me to a hidden sushi place on the Upper East Side, and he was so proud of himself for discovering it that I just didn't have the heart to tell him that, unlike every other person under forty in Manhattan, I cannot stand sushi. Big mistake. I spent the entire meal trying to choke down mouthfuls of seaweed and salmon by telling myself it was pizza. I didn't hear a word that guy said, and surprise surprise, he never called me again.

Any women's magazine will tell you not to wear new pumps to an interview. Why? Because they're uncomfortable, unpredictable, and can detract from the main event—you. Likewise, the most important thing on a first date is that you feel comfortable enough to be yourself. If you are yourself in a brand-new, hip restaurant with chrome interiors and a plate-to-food ratio of twenty to one, go for it. But if the local bistro is more your speed, that's fine, too. There will be time enough for him to take you out to fancy meals and parties in the future.

## Drive Him Crazy

Those of us who date in Manhattan have to deal with plenty of relationship hazards, but deciding whether or not the guy will pick us up before a first date is thankfully not one of them. For those of you who live outside the land of the yellow cab, navigating the rules of the road can be a bit trickier. Some things to bear in mind:

1. If you've met him only once in a bar or at the gym, take separate cars and meet him at the restaurant. This is the safest approach and allows for an easy out should things not go according to plan.

2. If you know him semi-well or you have mutual friends and he offers to pick you up at home, let him do so as long as you're comfortable with it. This is a chance for him to make a good impression—or not. There's no excuse for him not to come to your door. Any guy who's still beeping the horn to signal his arrival after moving on from his learner's permit is not fit to be dating. Bonus points if he opens the car door for you.

3. The interior of a man's car shows how serious he is about impressing you. If he offers to pick you up, but does so in a car that's full of Dr Pepper cans and Snickers wrappers, it may not be a deal breaker, but it's not a great sign.

4. People reveal their true colors in the car. Frustration, bossiness, and anxiety can all be disguised over a nice pasta dinner and a bottle of Chianti, but his behavior (and yours) will likely be less diluted as you drive together. If you have any bad car habits (this means you, Ms. Backseat Driver), try to keep them in check while out on a date with someone whom you don't know all that well.

## Restaurant Etiquette

You can tell a lot about a man from the way he acts in a restaurant. Snapping fingers to get the waiter's attention? Deal breaker. Tucking his napkin into his shirt when he's not eating lobster? See ya, buddy. Better luck next time. Chances are, he's paying attention to the way you behave, too. Some things to bear in mind:

- **Where should you put your purse?** Miss Manners advises that you place it in your lap (so bring a small one) and tuck it under your napkin. If you get up to use the bathroom, put it (and the napkin) on your chair.

- **Table settings.** Flatware is placed around the plate in the order in which you will use it (from the outside in). Use the fork and knife farthest from the plate for salad, the next ones for appetizers, and so on.

- **Don't cut your bread.** The correct way to eat dinner rolls, or any bread that's served at the table, is to break it apart with your hands.

- **Used silverware.** Never put it down on the tablecloth. Instead, place the knife and fork side by side in the upper left-hand part of your plate (at the eleven o'clock position).

- **As God is my witness, please never go hungry (on a date) again.** When doing research for this book (i.e., having lots of free meals with wealthy men), I discovered a disturbing fact—apparently, tons of women actually carry out the cliché of eating only a side salad on a first date. I thought everyone had gotten the memo by now that men find it disturbing when you do this. As one guy put it, "How am I supposed to impress her with a fancy dinner when she orders a garden salad and a glass of tap water?" For the love of womankind, please eat something. And not a celery stick.

## Don't Drink and Date

One first-date faux pas that you simply *must* avoid is getting drunk. Don't starve yourself all afternoon before dinner so your stomach looks flat in your new black pants. You may be an Atkins girl, but before a date you should carbo-load like you're running a marathon the next day. Once you're at the restaurant, reach for the breadbasket, and eat an entrée that is rich in protein, like chicken, with a green, leafy salad. Remember that a twelve-ounce beer is about 4 percent alcohol, a four-ounce glass of wine is 15 to 20 percent alcohol, and a shot of hard liquor can be up to 50 percent alcohol. Stick with white wine and avoid mixed drinks if you think you'll be tempted to have more than one or two.

Excessive drinking is a leading cause of cringe-worthy date behavior, but even more important, it's unsafe. Don't match your date drink for drink. His body will metabolize alcohol much faster than yours, and after four rounds he might still be relatively sober, while you are waxing poetic about the one that got away. Try to alternate each drink with a full glass of water, and don't worry that he's thinking you're a lightweight—chances are, he won't even notice. Besides, have you ever heard any man say "I knew she was the one when I saw how easily she could throw back seven margaritas in a sitting"?

## Top Ten Conversation Topics to Avoid on a First Date

We've already covered what you should talk about. Over dinner with the five most quality men I know—two Wall Street bankers, a lawyer, a teacher, and a private investor—I asked what they thought were the absolute worst topics a girl could raise on a first date. Here's what they said:

1. **Don't open the ex files.** Every single guy I asked mentioned this one. I can't say it enough—no matter what, no matter why, *do not* mention former boyfriends, crushes, etc.

2. **OR the sex files.** Why do some women insist on talking about previous conquests with the new men in their lives? Trust me, he doesn't think it's sexy that you once kissed a girl after too many piña coladas in college, or that you and your ex liked to do it on the roof of his building. Would you want to hear about the best sex he ever had? Okay, enough said.

3. **Don't talk about the future.** Even if you've already paired your last name with his, you'll only freak him out if you employ too much we-speak. Instead of saying "Oh, we have to go to the Met next weekend," say

"There's a new exhibit I'm dying to see." Let him say he's interested, too.

4. **Don't get too serious.** So your father was just laid off for the second time this year, or your uncle was diagnosed with cancer. As heartless as it sounds, it's best to keep tales of your personal tragedy to a minimum on a first date. A lot of women think that a date is a chance to be emotionally intimate. As we've discussed, a first date should be more like a job interview—you should be personable but not overly personal. It's a chance to speak in a friendly way, get to know about him, and show off your best assets. Skeletons should be like sneakers on a first date: keep them in the closet, where they belong.

5. **Don't talk about money, and don't act enamored of his wealth.** Instead, use subtle ways of finding out how much he's worth. Ask where he spent summers as a kid, about the eating club he was in at Princeton, where he went to camp, which church his family goes to, etc. *Do not* say anything along the lines of "Holy crap, you had dinner with the Clintons?" If you want him to start picturing you as a future partner, he'll have to think you're confident and grounded enough to take fame and fortune in stride.

6. **Don't say anything disparaging about your family, friends, or boss.** You may think it's bringing you closer, but it's not. Don't assume he's a fixture, so he should know now about your crazy Aunt Mildred. Instead,

think of this as your one chance to make a great first impression, and be as positive as you can.

7. **Don't mention how piddly (or impressive) your salary is.** Telling him how much you make is not cute. It's crass. Quality rich men don't talk about money, but they are aware that certain women see them as walking dollar signs. By setting yourself off as poorer than him, you'll be inadvertently sending up a red flag in his head. On the flip side, by talking about your amazing income, you might intimidate him.

8. **Don't fight over the bill.** He pays. End of story. If you so desire, there will be occasions for you to buy him dinner in the future (may I suggest your twentieth wedding anniversary?).

9. **Don't talk about how close you are with your mother.** Apparently this freaks guys out. I'm not exactly sure why, but after one banker told me this, I started asking other guys, and they all concurred. They don't want to think about you and your mom having late-night chats about them, I guess. Personally, I find this one a bit odd. And when I told my mother about it, she was downright perplexed. Just kidding, guys.

10. **Don't talk about getting ready.** Almost every man on the planet says he wants a low-maintenance girl who doesn't wear makeup. But they have no idea who's wearing makeup and who isn't. Why make it your job to tell them?

## Paying

As previously stated, don't argue about paying the bill. But don't act like you assume he's going to pay it, either. Paying on dates, especially first dates, used to be clean-cut. Now there's a lot of sensitivity about it in some places (if you're dating down South or in the Midwest, you can go ahead and skip this section). So here are the moves: Make one attempt to pay—reach for your purse, or perhaps even pull out a credit card. This lets your date know that you're independent and that you're not using him for his money. After he shoos your card away, thank him politely for dinner, and move on. If he doesn't shoo your card away, simply pay for your half and never speak to him again.

## Goodnight, Sweetheart, Well, It's Time to Go . . .

No first date should last longer than four or five hours. If you meet him at seven for dinner, make sure you are well on your way home by midnight. Think of yourself like Cinderella. You need to get your Volkswagen Jetta back into the driveway before it turns into a pumpkin, or you make a fool of yourself—whichever comes first. Even if you are having the time of your life, force yourself to say good-bye. Men like mystery and a bit of a challenge. If he thinks he's learned everything there is to know about you by the end of the date, the chances of him calling again will decrease.

And if you go home with him, the chances will pretty much cease to exist. Remember that great old love song

"Wouldn't It Be Nice?" by the Beach Boys? Well, when the Beach Boys sang, "It's gonna make it that much better, when we can say goodnight and stay together," they were:

a. Boys.

b. Not trying to marry a quality man.

No matter how much fun you are having, no matter what a fantastic guy he is, and no matter how much he begs, *never spend the night with someone after only one date.* This may seem old-fashioned or too prescribed, but let me tell you—I am very much of the mind-set that the When to Have Sex question should be decided on a case-by-case basis. Any third-date, fifth-date, or (in the case of one particularly dedicated woman I know) eighteenth-date rule seems silly to me. You're an independent woman. You can decide when you're ready. However, in the experience of every woman I know, no good has ever come of taking someone home after the first date. It causes confusion to even the most practical of women, and frankly, it doesn't give him the best impression of you.

The proper way to say goodnight is as follows: If he leans in to kiss you and it feels right, by all means let him. But by "kiss," I mean a *kiss*—a brief, sweet exchange, rather than a makeout scene worthy of an MTV dating show. If you've enjoyed yourself, as an assertive, vocal woman, you might very well wish to ask him when you'll see him again. Resist this urge with all your might. Especially in the beginning, it's essential to leave him guessing about just how interested you are. Tell him you had a great time, and if he asks when he can see you again, say, "Soon, I hope. Give me a call."

If you play hard to get, I promise he'll come get you.

## Bouncing Back from a First-Date Fiasco

When I lived in London, I went on a first date with a banker named Marc whom I'd met at a cocktail party a few nights earlier. I had the perfect little black skirt picked out. The only trouble was, it didn't work with any of my shoes, so the morning before the date I bought a cheap pair of pumps in Camden Town. Marc and I agreed to meet in Covent Garden. When I reached the tube stop exit, I saw him waiting across the road. As I walked toward him our eyes met—and I proceeded to trip on a cobblestone and fall facedown in the crowded street, with my cute little black skirt up around my waist and my not quite so cute white cotton underwear on display for all to see. (Sidenote: does life imitate chick lit, or does chick lit imitate life?)

Why am I telling you this story, other than because it makes me look so damn cool? I'm telling you because, against all odds (and with the help of a couple strong gin and tonics), Marc and I actually had a pretty great time that night. Everyone's nervous on a first date, which means that embarrassment is more likely than ever to occur. Here's how to deal with some of the most common types of first-date fiasco.

**If you're late.** Despite your best efforts to always be on time, occasionally you just can't control the factors that make you run late—your boss asks for one last thing, your car gets stuck in traffic on the highway, your TiVo's broken, and there's no way you're missing the season finale of *America's Next Top*

*Model.* Whatever the reason, being late for a first date is stressful. If you're late by only five minutes or so, apologize once on your arrival, and then let it go. If you're ten minutes late, it's probably best to call him and let him know, but again, it's not a huge deal. Fifteen minutes or more requires a phone call and an enthusiastic apology once you get there. But don't act flustered or overly repentant—apologize, make a joke, and move on. And be prompt next time.

**If he brings up a personal topic.** Just because you are Breezy McBreezerson and wouldn't dream of getting too personal on a first date doesn't mean that he's the same way. I once met a young lawyer (a friend of a friend) for beers after work. Fifteen minutes into our conversation, when he should have been asking what my favorite movies were, he began talking about the history of manic depression in his family. Fifteen minutes after *that,* he was literally crying into his Heineken and repeating the sentence "I just hate my father." If a man launches into his personal tragedies on a first date, it's okay to act sympathetic, but try to change the subject. Don't encourage him to go on about it—you're his date, not his therapist (or even his girlfriend). It is my experience that there are many men who say too much in the beginning, leading the women they're dating to assume that they are emotionally wide open. Not so. Most often, these guys get freaked by their own openness and never make it to date number three anyway. Whatever you do, don't take it as an invitation to start talking about your own personal life. Once again, remember the job interview scenario. Over-sharing has no place on a first date. Imagine if you were at a job interview and your would-be boss started sobbing. This would be your cue to walk out the door and complain to HR, not to grab a box of tissues and join in.

**If you put your foot in your mouth.** Humor is a vital part of handling all of life's major stresses—work, debt, illness, and (coming in right at the top of the list) first dates. A woman I know once went on a date with a guy from her office, and halfway into dinner she made a joke about the vice president of their company, whose name is Sid—"In our department, we've decided that SID stands for self-important dirtbag," she laughed. Her date turned pale. "Sid's my uncle," he said. Not missing a beat, my friend said, "And they call me SBATS. Stands for Shouldn't Be Allowed To Speak." Luckily, her date laughed, and they carried on as if nothing had happened. Most guys are willing to overlook a conversational faux pas if you call attention to it, but don't make it seem like a big deal.

**If you spill something on yourself.** If you're the kind of girl who tends to cut calories by dropping half of your dinner onto your sweater, carry Shout wipes in your purse on a first date. After a spill, excuse yourself, and try to flag down a waiter or busboy on your way to the bathroom to see if he can give you a little white vinegar. Blot the stain (don't rub!) with the Shout wipes, removing any excess sauce or liquid that hasn't sunken in yet, then blend tepid water with a few drops of the vinegar (or just use the water on its own if vinegar isn't available). Dry the stain under a hand dryer. Sometimes it's not possible to remove a stain completely—a glass of Shiraz down the front of your white silk camisole is best left to the dry cleaners. But again, laughter can see you through. Just say "Oh well. People always tell me I look good in red."

**If you run into an ex.** Despite the common fantasy of running into your ex while out with a new guy, it can still be scary and off-putting—especially if you're on a first date. Remember that there's a reason you're not with him anymore, and that (for tonight at least) you should be most interested in making sure your date is having a good time. Say hello to your ex if you must, but keep it short and sweet. Once you've parted ways, it's okay to be honest and say "We used to date," if your new guy asks (especially if your ex is hot—hey, a little healthy competition is good for a man), but do not take his presence as a sign to start talking about him or where your relationship went wrong. Save it for the post-date wrap-up call with your best friend.

**If he says something offensive.** On a first date, two relative strangers try one another on for size. Sometimes what feels like an awkward fit can actually be comfortable if you give it a chance. Each one of us has a distinct set of values and beliefs, and it's important to know what you can and cannot tolerate in another person. But it's also important to give the guy a chance and consider where he's coming from. I once got into a heated debate about pornography on a first date (note to self: *never* do that again), and stormed out of the restaurant. This was totally immature and uncalled for, as my date was only expressing his (utterly wrong, but whatever) opinion, and was very open to hearing mine. However, on another ill-fated first date, when the guy uttered a racial slur about someone in the restaurant, I proceeded to tell him that I wouldn't tolerate that ignorant language, splashed my gin and tonic in his face, and walked out the door. Even years later, I'm still glad I did that. Pick your battles. Take everything with a grain of salt, but don't be afraid to cut things short and stand your ground if you feel he's crossed a line. You wouldn't want to go out with him again anyway—and every woman should have the chance to throw a drink in a man's face at least once in her life.

**If you accidentally get drunk.** Despite the fact that you ate plenty of tortilla chips and sipped each one of your eight mojitos over dinner, you still got drunk. Switch to water and, if you have a propensity to get drunk on dates, write yourself a note ahead of time and stick it in your purse. Include a list of commands for your intoxicated self, such as *Do not go home with him, Do not talk too much, Do not get on the bar and start dancing along to Britney Spears songs,* or whatever embarrassing behavior you're likely to enact. You can also pre-arrange a phone call with a friend who knows to tell you to stop drinking, and write CALL SARAH (or whatever her name is) on the list as a reminder. It's probably also a good idea to write GO HOME NOW down, because if you're more than tipsy on a first date, no good will come of it. As soon as you know you've had one drink too many (I can always tell because I start singing show tunes in the bathroom), excuse yourself and read the note. You'll have to be your own sober best friend, which means getting yourself home before you do anything cringe-worthy. Of course, there are times when even the smartest girls among us just don't listen to the designated note writer. If you get drunk and make an ass out of yourself, all you can do is send an apologetic e-mail the next day and move on.

**If he refuses to pay or doesn't have enough money.** My Aunt Nancy (a successful lawyer who is married to another successful lawyer) has given me lots of dating advice over the years. Since I was in high school, she's been telling me never to pay on a first date. It wasn't until I graduated from college that I realized why. When a man pays, it's a polite gesture, a customary kindness. It has nothing to do with your inability to pay for your own meal (if you bought those Manolos you're wearing, you can buy yourself a steak) and everything to do with his manners. Aunt Nancy's most memorable story on this topic is about a guy she calls Wrinkled Pants Man. WPM showed up for their first and only date dressed sloppily, in a T-shirt and, you guessed it, wrinkled pants. He had nothing interesting to say, didn't ask her a thing about herself, and when the check arrived, he proceeded to pull a roll of dollar bills from his pocket and count them out one by one on the table before announcing that he didn't have enough money. Aunt Nancy has guts of steel, so she simply directed him to the nearest ATM three blocks away and waited while he took out more cash. If you can make that kind of statement, by all means do. Personally, I would have pulled out my credit card as soon as the money roll surfaced. In any case, as previously stated, if your date doesn't at least offer to pay, send him packing.

# Going the Distance

"How poor are they who have not patience!"

—William Shakespeare

So the first date went off without a hitch. You like the same books, you own all the same DVDs, you both want three kids, you're both dog people. Now what? This chapter will help you navigate the rest—from those early dates, to your first interactions with his friends and parents, to saying "I do." The main thing to remember, especially early in the relationship, is to go slow, sexually, emotionally, and mentally. Think of a new man like a baby deer in the woods. He's cute, he's sweet, and he is going to bolt in the other direction if you act too quickly.

Dates two, three, and four should carry on in much the same manner as the first if you're serious about marriage. These days, thanks to *Sex and the City* and chick lit novels, many women can't imagine how *not* to take a guy home with them after only one or two dates. They're afraid he will lose interest or see them as prudish. Or, in a lot of cases, they just want to sleep with him. But as my friend Karin says, if you two are in it for the long haul, eighty years from now you'll be doing little else besides staring across a table, talking to each other, so it's probably best to figure out if you can do that now, before jumping into bed.

It's also best to stay in semi-interview mode for the first month. Not that you have to act like some kind of Stepford Wife. Be yourself, but hold back a little. He's not your boyfriend yet. You're still trying each other on for size. So no uber-serious conversations, no making of future plans, and no state-of-the-union talks about where the relationship is going. I know what you're thinking. No sex *and* no drama? Now what the hell are you supposed to do together? How about getting to know each other for real and getting a true sense of whether this is something you want to pursue.

A few other things to bear in mind during the first month:

**Don't see him more than once a week.** Sure, you're crazy about him. You can't stop thinking about him. All you want to do is talk to him, and you're certain he feels the same way. This is great news, but not a reason to bring your social life to a screaming halt. Never cancel plans that are already in place to do something with him—this sets up too much dependency on your relationship too soon, and is a crappy thing to do to your friends. Also, it's good to seem unavailable, especially at first. Remember, dumb as it sounds, men like a challenge. If you don't have plans that don't include him, make some (or make some up).

**Don't call him more than he calls you.** It's the day after your second date and you're watching *Bridget Jones: The Edge of Reason* on DVD when you realize how much his eyes look like Hugh Grant's. You're dying to call him, just to say hi . . . You're driving along the highway and you see the new football stadium they're building, the one he told you about over dinner. You consider dialing his number to tell him that he was correct—it *does* look like an egg . . . During the first month, you might find yourself longing to pick up the phone and hear his voice several times a day. Do not do it. It's okay to return his calls, or to initiate a conversation if it's just to make plans. Otherwise, tell him the pressing news the next time you see him. And while we're on the subject of phone calls, let's take a second to discuss the number one killer of new relationships—drunk dialing. If you have a propensity to drink and dial when you're out with friends (you know who you are), choose a designated dialer at the beginning of the night. This should be your most hard-assed (or your most sober) friend present. Give her your guy's number, erase it from your phone (including from your incoming, missed, and outgoing call lists, as drunk dialers can be crafty), and instruct her not to give it to you until Sunday brunch no matter what you say.

**Don't use him as your emotional crutch.** One of the best parts of having a great boyfriend is that he's there for you when you're down. He brings you chicken soup when you're sick, he listens to you rant when your boss takes credit for your work, he's on your side in every argument you have with your mother. So why not expect a guy to do these things after three or four fabulous dates? Because he's not your boyfriend yet. Sometimes women get so caught up in the idea of someone, that they never take the time to see who he is. Don't treat an individual like your new emotional catchall. That will come later, naturally, if he's right for you.

**Keep the talking about him to a minimum.** You think it's adorable that he pronounces Boston "Bahhston," and that he still sleeps with his baby blanket. Let me remind you of something I learned about women back in the eighth grade, when girls congregated in the bathroom during school dances to exchange stories about the stupid boys who had stepped on their feet, or tried to get to second base during "Tears in Heaven," or sweated all over their jean jackets. For the most part, we only like to hear about one another's boyfriends when there's bitching and complaining involved. Recounting your entire afternoon in the park with him would be like recounting an entire episode of *The Cosby Show* scene for scene. If your friend didn't see it herself, it's just not going to be that funny or interesting to her. And rehashing the details of a date or phone conversation with him isn't healthy, even if it seems that you are genetically programmed to do it, because it heightens the importance of what transpired. Tell the story about him growing up in Capri once, twice, three times, and it becomes larger than life, a new story evolves from the telling. Treat evenings out with him like evenings out with any other friend. Experience what it's like to be with him, and remember the feeling, but don't become obsessed with the details.

## Let's Get It On

You've been together for a month or two. You're going to have sex with him. Maybe not today, maybe not tomorrow, but soon and (hopefully) for the rest of your life. It's old-fashioned and a little bit manipulative, but try to wait as long as you can to sleep with him if you're serious about having a future together. Four weeks is the absolute minimum, but eight to twelve is even better.

What's the best way to do it once you are ready? Well, that's up to you. I'm not a big fan of magazines, books, or television shows that offer sexual instruction—the mechanics should be pretty obvious, and everything else is a matter of personal preference. (Although, come over to my apartment with a pitcher of sangria and ask me to describe the corner canoodle position if you're ever looking for inspiration. Really, ladies. It's a show-stopper.)

Still, there's a lot to be learned about sex beyond the basics. What can you do to knock a guy's socks off the first few times? How can you separate yourself out from the rest of the pack? And is there anything you can do to utterly kill the mood? To answer these and other pressing questions, I got the oven warmed up and the wine corked, and invited a bunch of boys over for dinner.

(Side note: I totally recommend writing a dating book if

you want to know what all the men in your life think about relationships. I can't believe the things guys will tell me in the name of research. Okay, moving on.)

Things he's not thinking about:

- **Your physical flaws.** "It kills me when a girl says something disparaging about her body during sex, or when she insists on turning the lights off because she feels fat," says Dave, an accountant. Men like naked women, and the vast majority of them would prefer a little bit of curve (or even a lot of curve) to none at all. Men like looking at women, and they like having sex. They're not out to judge your figure or gossip about your cellulite. Relax. And stop sucking in. Focus on your own pleasure, and you'll increase his as well.

- **Your messy apartment.** "I had been dating this girl for about a month, and finally the night came when we were going to sleep together," my friend Ed told me. "We're lying in her bed, we start making out, and she keeps saying, 'Sorry it's so dusty in here. I can't believe how dusty it is. I just vacuumed.' It was the weirdest thing. She was probably just nervous, but it brought the energy of the night down a lot." Umm, come on now. Compared to the sight of you naked, a few dust bunnies will not even register. And on that note, another thing he's definitely not thinking about . . .

- **How much he loves your La Perla negligee, white Diptyque candles, and four-hundred-thread-count sheets.**

An editor friend of mine put it best: "No candles, please. Nothing says 'this means more to me than it does to you' like candles." The consensus among the men I interviewed seems to be that any extra props you want to add to the equation are fine (and in some cases, more than fine), but only as long as you actually like them and you aren't forcing it. Paul, a doctor, said, "Some girls can work the lingerie, but with others you can just tell that they feel stupid, like a Saint Bernard with a pink bow on its head. The guy just wants to have sex. He doesn't care what you're wearing while you do it."

- **His ex-girlfriend.** Women of the world, I have to say it: sometimes I am embarrassed on behalf of us all. Every man I spoke to said that at least once in his dating career, he's had a woman ask about one of his exes and how she compares sexually, while they were in bed together. There's nothing to say about this except *eww,* please don't do it.

- **That you are now totally and officially together.** We've all heard this eight hundred times, but it bears repeating (in caps)—SEX MEANS DIFFERENT THINGS TO MEN AND WOMEN. Though sleeping together might mean a new level of intimacy for both of you, he's not thinking that he loves you all the more because you finally did the deed.

What he *is* thinking: Yippee, someone is having sex with me.

## The All-Stars

Across the board, there are certain things that men told me drive them crazy (in a good way). Here's what they want you to know.

**Make noise.** Silence may be golden in some situations, but sex ain't one of 'em. Making noise helps him know when he's pleasing you, and adds to the overall sensory enjoyment of the situation. Feel free to moan, scream, and say exactly what you want him to do. You don't have any trouble opening your mouth and voicing your opinions outside of the bedroom. Why should things be any different between the sheets?

**Get involved.** The best sex isn't learned from watching porn or old Sharon Stone movies. The best sex is an extension of who you are in real life. You're a go-getter. You make things happen. You assert your desires, you get what you want, and you aim to impress. Just lying there has no place in this equation. Move around, try different positions, offer suggestions, and don't be afraid of looking silly or not knowing what to do. It's sex, not a standardized test. There is no time limit, you're allowed to draw outside the lines, and there is most definitely more than one correct answer.

**Get on top.** Experimenting with different positions is clutch, but this one is an old favorite. According to the guys I talked to, some girls are reluctant to get up there. Don't be. It's better for you because it offers a lot of clitoral stimulation, and it's great for him because it offers a fab view of you. What's not to love?

**Go down.** As my sister once said to me when she was in middle school, "Who gives blow jobs? Blow jobs are gross." This seems to be a belief still held by many adult women. If oral sex makes you uncomfortable, don't worry. You should never do anything sexual that makes you feel weird. But that said, men dig it. I'm sure this comes as no surprise to you, but my team of experts made me promise I'd mention it.

**Take it outside the bedroom.** No, I don't mean have sex on the kitchen table (although that can be fun, too). I mean find ways of exciting him when you're not in the same room. Send him a sexy e-mail or text message in the middle of the day when he's not expecting it. A more sophisticated man will appreciate your efforts to stimulate his body *and* his mind.

## Keeping Quiet

Every week I have dinner with the most fabulous posse of gay men the West Village has ever known. They are bawdy and hilarious, and one of their favorite things to talk about is the number of sexual partners each of us has had. There is also a lot of sex talk at the table, and being of a certain "When in Rome" mentality, I always join right in. The only person who doesn't speak up is Joseph, a renowned hairstylist who's a bit older than the rest of the crowd, and a bit mellower (though he did a lot of partying at Studio 54 in his day). One night, as we paid the check, Joseph leaned toward me and whispered, "Honey, let me give you a piece of advice—it's all well and good for you to talk about this stuff with us, but when you meet a nice boy, zip your lip. If he asks you about your number, just laugh and be coy. Trust me, he doesn't want to know."

Joseph's point is a good one. There's no reason to trundle out all your glory stories. They'll make your man feel intimidated, stressed, and creeped out. Likewise, harping on *his* number isn't the best idea either. And please (do I have to say it?) don't ask him how you stack up against the others. A man who sees a future with you will never ask you about any of these things, and if you want to have a future with him, it's best if you follow suit.

## If the Sex Is Bad

This situation can be summed up by the tale of one unfortunate man whom my friend Allison dated. He had brains, money, a great family, and a Georgetown law degree. Until the third date, every woman we knew wished she had found him first. But then Allison went home with him, and the next day when she told the story over brunch, we christened him the Small-Penised Lawyer. Sounds mean, I know, but apparently it was a pretty apt name. There were acorn comparisons being made, people. So what's a girl to do when she meets the man of her dreams and then realizes that they have no chemistry in bed? Or that he's not equipped for the job? Before you break out your Patsy Cline CDs and declare your great relationship over, consider the following:

**Give it time.** Sex often gets better with time. As you grow more comfortable with each other, and more familiar with one another's bodies, you might see a big change. I remember a friend of mine calling me from the bathroom of her boyfriend's apartment after they'd slept together for the first time. "It was awful," she said, disappointed, almost on the verge of tears. "It was the worst sex of my life." Two years later, they are engaged. I asked her once after we'd downed a bottle of wine, if the sex had ever improved. "Oh, Lord, yes," she said. "I never would have married the guy if it had stayed like that." I asked her what had changed, and she told me that they'd just gotten used to one another and figured out positions that worked for both of them. So give it a little time if he's worth it, even if it's always come to you very naturally in the past. Sometimes you just have to work at it. And is it such a bad thing to have to practice? You made it through your childhood piano lessons unscathed. This should be no problem.

**Try new things.** Another friend of mine has what she calls a stringbean fetish. She likes her men long, lanky, and lean. So when she recently fell for a guy who might be more appropriate for a girl with a tomato fetish—he's short, round, and bald—we were all a bit surprised. No one was more surprised than her. She loved his sense of humor, his perfect manners, and his politics. But she was freaked out about sleeping with him. After all, she was used to having sex with guys who resembled basketball players, and this one resembled, well, an actual basketball. The first time they had sex, she reports, it was different from anything she'd experienced before. And not in a good way. He didn't have the muscles or the inclination toward throw-down that she was accustomed to, and that scared her. But after three or four times, she realized that this was going to be a new kind of sex. Sex where she played a more active role, sex where she was the teacher for once. Don't be afraid to try something new, and release your inhibitions. That is what good sex is all about.

**Don't panic.** Nothing is less sexy than stressing about sex. If you spend all of your time together thinking, *Oh my God, the sex is awful,* things aren't going to get very far. Instead, think of it as a challenge and confront it as you would any other—by rising to the occasion and remaining open to the possibility that it will work out.

**Say something.** Sometimes it's not about a small penis or getting to know one another's bodies. Sometimes the guy is just awful in bed. Of course, telling him this would be like telling a runway model that his fly was down for the entire spring show—even thinking about how mortified he would be makes you want to never bring it up, no matter what. But communication is the most important part of any relationship, and you're not going to get what you want unless you ask for it. Most guys are very responsive to, and even aroused by, your suggestions for how they can please you sexually. As long as you phrase things in a positive way (e.g., by saying "I love when you do that, but it makes me even crazier when you go slowly" rather than "Jeez, slow down there, it's not a goddamn triathlon"), he will most likely be into it. In the experience of every woman I know, men are not afraid of saying what they want us to do in bed (whether or not we take them up on it is a totally different story), and there's no reason why we should feel uncomfortable about doing the same.

## SECRET WEAPON: The Corner Canoodle

By now, you've probably guessed that I have a hard time keeping secrets. Remember what I said about the corner canoodle? Well, forget it. I will tell you, even without the sangria. One cold winter night back in college, a dorm mate of mine asked a table full of women in the King House dining hall what their favorite positions were. She got the standard fare of responses. Most were on-toppers (the official T-shirts for the Smith College centennial were printed with the phrase A CENTURY OF WOMEN ON TOP), a few liked missionary style, and so on.

"Anyone tried the corner canoodle?" she asked.

We were all intrigued. She described the position in detail. It was enough to draw our attention away from the sundae bar. In the weeks that followed, every girl at that table tried the corner canoodle, and every girl at that table found her new favorite position.

Here's how it works. The guy sits on the corner of the bed (the corner should form a triangle between his legs), with his feet planted firmly on the floor. He then lies back, so that he's lying flat on the bed (his feet still touching the floor.) Position yourself as if you were just getting on top—knees bent, lying over him. Once you're both in place, have him sit up, and wrap your legs around his lower back, so that your chests are touching. Grab hold of him, and go to town. The position works so darn well for a few reasons—it lets you get super close, provides a ridiculous amount of clitoral stimulation, and (depending on how strong his legs are), the movement of the bed intensifies the whole experience. (Just make sure that the bed is securely in place, and not on wheels. Otherwise it might tip over. Trust me on this one.)

If you haven't tried this position yet, put down the book and call your boyfriend. No need to thank me. As I learned in the dining hall that night back in college, the corner canoodle is too good to keep to yourself.

And now that my extended Irish Catholic family's collective jaw has hit the floor, let's move along.

## The "L" Word and Other Stressful Verbiage

When my last serious boyfriend and I were on our sixth or seventh date, I made a comment over brunch about how we were "dating." His face turned serious, and he said, "I wouldn't say we're dating. We're seeing each other." When I asked him what the difference was, he expounded on his theory that first you're seeing each other, then you're dating, then you're boyfriend/girlfriend and so on. For about three days, I tortured myself over this one. Why did I think we were dating each other, while he was still a phase behind? I whipped myself into a frenzy, and practically prepared a speech complete with flow charts and a PowerPoint presentation, determined to make him see it my way.

Then, thankfully, my sanity returned to me and I realized that it didn't matter. If a guy treats you well, and you're having fun together, don't freak out about definitions and labels in the beginning of a relationship. Even the most calm and rational of women have had the urge to scream "ARE YOU MY

BOYFRIEND OR WHAT?!" But try to resist it as long as you can. It's always better if he says it first.

As if the "Where is this going?" conversation isn't stressful enough, there's also the L bomb to contend with. Four little words comprise what is perhaps the most awkward of all dialogue exchanges:

"I love you."

"Thanks."

My friend Amy wanted to tell David, her boyfriend of four months, that she loved him. Everyone advised her to wait. It was a little soon, he was squeamish about commitment anyway, and (again) it's always better if the guy says it first.

But Amy was excited. She couldn't hold it in any longer. And in a scene straight out of a bad romantic comedy, she chose to deliver the news at a noisy outdoor concert. She tapped David on the shoulder, clutched his hand, and said, "I love you."

Naturally, he couldn't hear her over the music, and so he yelled, "What?"

"I love you," she said again, a little bit louder this time.

"What?!" he shouted, leaning in closer.

"I LOVE YOU!" she screamed, just as the song ended and silence fell over the park.

"Oh wow," David said, genuinely moved. "Thank you."

Amy was crushed, but a month later, when David finally said it, too, she felt that he meant it, and had come to the idea in his own time, rather than succumbing to pressure and saying something that wasn't true. Some men are very cautious about the L word. If you've already put it out there (or even if you haven't) and you're freaking out about why he can't say it, relax. It's important to find out *why* he's not saying it. And yes, you can ask him. I've had guys tell me that they loved me after two dates. And I've had guys wait for six months. Using words (especially loaded words like "love") to describe feelings is difficult, because not everyone ascribes the same meaning to a given word. Some men have said "I love you" to every girl they've ever dated, as a sort of shorthand for saying "I sure like having you around." Others plan to say it only to the girl they're going to marry. So go ahead and ask him where he falls on the spectrum. Of course, if he says, "I don't love you, and I don't think I ever will," it's probably time to call it a day. But if he explains that he's just not ready yet, or that it's coming, but it might take a while, accept what he says and stop obsessing. Love is just a word. What's most important is the way he treats you. Base your evaluation of the relationship on that.

You graduated summa cum laude from Barnard, you passed the Bar Exam on your first try, and you've never lost a case, no matter how tough the judge was. Yet choosing a present for your boyfriend seems like the most daunting task you've ever undertaken. A few preliminary tips—most important, don't break the bank just because he has money. As a doctor friend told me, "I can buy my own Ferrari, and my own sound system. When a woman gives me a gift, I don't want her spending tons of cash—it's nice to know she's thinking of me, but something too ostentatious is embarrassing." That said, thoughtful doesn't mean giving him a copy of *Pat the Bunny* because he once told you that it was his favorite book as a kid, or buying him a big stuffed teddy bear to sleep with when you're out of town. He's a dude. What do you expect him to do with gifts that are suitable for a four-year-old girl? Also, sexist as it may seem, Valentine's Day is for women. Don't give him a big satin heart full of chocolates or send him flowers at work. If you must do something, bake him a tart or take him out for brunch. The only time you should be giving him a gift is on a major holiday like Christmas or Hanukkah, or on his birthday. If the gift-giving gods are smiling on you, your birthday will fall before his does, so you'll be able to gauge what you should give him based on what he gave you. If fate is not so kind, follow these guidelines.

**If you've been dating for six months or less.** The first six months are the hardest ones in which to buy your man a gift, because your relationship is probably changing from one week to the next. Cologne makes a great gift for your boyfriend of four months or longer. (If he already has a signature scent, try giving him something else from the same line—aftershave, body lotion, or soap. Or you can take his scent to a perfumer, and ask for something different with similar notes so you can be sure he'll like it.) But it will likely scare a guy off if you buy it for him after only a few weeks. If you've been seeing each other for less than a month and your relationship has not yet reached boyfriend-girlfriend status, it's best just to take him out for dinner, and provide no physical present. During the second and third months, it's okay to give him some token, as long as it's not at all romantic. Alcohol is good. A nice bottle of his favorite liquor or a bottle of wine from his birth year and two glasses makes a nice gesture. A book you've been talking about or tickets to a sporting event work well, too. At this stage, in general, limit yourself to fifty dollars and gifts that don't reek of "we'll be together forever and for always" (i.e., a framed portrait of you, or your grandfather's pocket watch).

**If you've been dating for six months to a year.** Once you've been together for a while longer, it's okay to venture into giving gifts that have a more permanent feeling. Clothing is good, since most men hate shopping for themselves, but buy him something that he will like, not the pink button-down you've been nagging him to try. My friend Lauren recently bought her boyfriend a jigsaw for his birthday (he's one serious handyman in his spare time). When I made a joke about how unromantic the gift was, she said, "I've been down that monogrammed money clip and cuff links road before. Guys don't really want that stuff." The girl has a point. If your man has been in relationships in the past, he likely has a whole drawer of monogrammed cuff links. They're sort of the boyfriend equivalent of giving your dad a tie for Father's Day. Why not get him a gift that shows you know and care about his interests.

**If you've been dating for a year or more.** If you have the financial resources, it's okay to up the ante a little bit after a year—but still resist the urge to buy him a Jaguar, even if he tends to go all out on your birthday. Not everything in the relationship needs to be equal, and gifts are one area where the man should be putting in a little more effort than you. (If this notion irks you, just remember—he will never give birth to your child.)

As with the first gift you ever gave him, be thoughtful. If his lifelong dream is to learn how to make a perfect soufflé, send him to cooking classes. If he loves flying, take him on a helicopter ride. Ultimately, no matter what relationship stage you're at, remember that men are different from women in a lot of ways. They aren't going to infer anything about you or your relationship from a gift. They're just going to think it's cool (see tickets to a sporting event) or not (see *Pat the Bunny*).

## Getting to Know His Friends

There comes a time in every new relationship when you begin to feel utterly secure around one another. You're comfortable with silence as you read the paper together over breakfast, you finish each other's sentences, you give him the spare key. The hard part is over. Right? Fat chance. Oh, my dears, this is only the beginning. Sure, you've proven yourself to him, but now you'll have to prove that you're a keeper to his friends and family. A certain level of decorum and formality is necessary when you're with his parents—we'll get to that. Friends are harder, because they're not likely to be swayed by your impeccable breeding or your offer to clear the dishes after brunch. They will be more concerned with your personality, and sometimes it can be intimidating to try to prove what a great catch you are to a whole new group of people.

To determine the best strategy for making his friends fall in love with you, I once again summoned a gaggle of rich men to my apartment for dinner and grilled them on the topic. What were some things a girl could do to wow their friends? What were some surefire ways she could shoot herself in the foot? What success stories did they have to tell? Was there a formula?

The men I invited over were all very different—the charming investment banker, the well-bred foreign consultant, the sweet but shy book editor, the party boy Canadian heir, the cutthroat attorney, the totally nerdy (sorry, Matt) pediatrician. But all of their answers were similar, regardless of their jobs or personalities. Maybe it was the company, or maybe it was the free-flowing cheap wine. Whatever the case, those boys talked. Here's the best of what they had to say.

**Meet his friends in small groups or one-on-one.** Even the most extroverted of girlfriends might cringe at the thought of having to meet all of her man's friends at once. Meeting them in small groups can relieve some of the pressure and give you a chance to actually get to know them. As Harry, a consultant in San Francisco, put it, "Your new girlfriend isn't going to respond and act the same way she normally does if there are a billion new people around, so she will probably come off differently to friends if you try to force them all on her at once. And first impressions mean a lot, so you don't want everyone thinking she's shy or boring. It's always been best for me if a girl meets my friends gradually."

**Don't orchestrate a "meet my best friends" night.** Last summer, my friend Nora was so excited about a guy she'd been out with twice that she sent a mass e-mail to her ten nearest and dearest entitled "Come Meet My Future Husband." She set up a get-together at her apartment in Soho for later that week, and we all arrived right on time because, crazy as she is, we wanted to support her (or maybe it was because she makes killer meatballs, I can't remember). Her man rang the bell fifteen minutes later, and as Nora went to answer the door, she hissed at our friend Jake, "By the way, he thinks this is a party for you, so don't be surprised if he says 'Happy birthday.'" Needless to say, it was an awkward night. Her guy felt like he was on display, because, well, he was. Don't orchestrate an evening that's all about parading your man around in front of your friends, and definitely don't let him do that to you. According to my friend James, "Introducing her during a social event like a birthday party and not just at some 'meet the girlfriend night' took the pressure off. It's best if it's just spontaneous that you brought her, and not this drawn-out 'tonight's the night!' routine. A big formal introduction just adds too much pressure."

**It is right to remain silent (if you hate his friends).** Unlike you, your man doesn't talk to his friends eight times a day, or end phone calls with them by saying "Love you, sweetie." But chances are, he has more allegiance to them than he does to you. "I hate it when women jump to conclusions about my friends right off the bat," says Rich, a real-estate developer. "I'm friends with them for a reason. If you meet them for five minutes, and automatically assume that they suck, I'm probably going to think there's something wrong with you. Give it a little while, and if you still can't stand his friends, at least you'll be able to back up your dislike with something other than a gut feeling, and then you can say that you gave it an honest try."

**Don't ask about your man's past.** When you meet his friends for the first time, there are a million things to talk about, but his personal information is not one of them. "Every man—and woman, for that matter—I know thinks it's annoying as hell if the girl starts asking everyone about her boyfriend's past," says Jacob, a book editor. "Either he'll tell you if he wants you to know, or if you end up becoming friends with his friends later, then they'll tell you. But in the beginning, they're his friends and it's just weird to assume they're going to turn state's witness on him."

**Don't act like a princess.** Maybe when it's just the two of you, you make him give you manicures and talk about feelings, but let the poor guy maintain a little bit of respect in front of his friends: "If a girl wants to impress my friends, the simplest thing she can do is order a beer," James says. "Nothing says 'I don't have my head up my ass' more than just getting a beer. I'm not saying she should shotgun a can of Pabst Blue Ribbon, but she should not be ordering an apple martini at the local pub."

(Sorry, appletini enthusiasts, but this next one is from a different guy. Survey says your favorite drink is best reserved for girls' night out . . .)

Jacob again: "Things she must not do: order an apple martini, complain about her uncomfortable shoes, cling to your side and not talk to anyone else, denigrate your friends. Oh, and under no circumstances should she refer to you as her 'friend,' 'boyfriend,' or any other title, because that's just awkward. Referring to you simply by your name should suffice for those first few outings."

**Don't stand by your man all night long.** When you meet your new man's friends, you are under pressure to impress both him and them. This can lead you to mentally revert to the first day of kindergarten, when you hid inside your father's coat rather than confront all those new faces. But treat meeting his friends like you would the friends of a coworker or buddy of your own. "A lot of whether or not she gets along with your friends is luck of the draw personality-wise, but she should also just try to act natural and talk to them," says Rob, a film producer. "Don't be closed off or uptight and only enter conversations when your boyfriend or someone else invites you. Initiate conversations with a variety of people, and talk about things other than how you met their friend, where you went on your first date, etc." A word of caution from James: "This one girl I dated was so stuck to my side that we gave her the nickname Sir Clings-a-Lot. I had a big party, and she basically sat in a chair all night and only talked to people when they approached her. That wasn't cool. As intimidating as they might seem, his friends are just people, and you should be able to strike up a conversation with them."

**Be yourself.** Your boyfriend has chosen to be with you and introduce you to his friends because he likes you. So relax. Put your true self forward, and don't worry about what they think. You may adore each other from the start, or you may never understand what he sees in them. Either way, as long as you're kind and honest with his friends, everything will be fine. "Usually I think one way a girl can automatically get in good with her boyfriend's male friends is if she knows a thing or two about sports," says Karl, a law student. "That said, my wife is clueless about anything athletic. The first time she met my college buddies, we went to a football game, and she kept disappearing for long stretches of time to get beers or play arcade games, and then showing up and asking if the halftime show was about to start, since that's her favorite part. She acted like a total goon, but she was also acting comfortable, like she would if it were just the two of us there. By being herself, she won my friends over."

## His Female Friends

Never before have men and women occupied the same social sphere in the way we do now. We attend the same colleges, we work in the same offices, we hang out with members of the opposite sex whom we have no interest in dating, in groups, or one-on-one. Having straight male friends is fabulous (without straight male friends, I couldn't have written this book), but sometimes those relationships are hard to navigate. I can't count the number of times I've had a female friend ask me "Do you think this is a date?" when some coworker or friend asked her to dinner. Why do I feel like my grandmother never had this problem? Chances are, your new boyfriend has some friends who are girls, maybe even really close ones.

My ex had a best friend who—seriously, no hyperbole here—looked like Barbie. She had the longest legs I have ever seen, a ridiculous mane of blond hair, and perhaps the perkiest natural breasts on this planet. She was the kind of woman who got hit on when she went to the grocery store in sweatpants and an overcoat. In addition to this, she was a guy's girl. She liked playing pool and darts at the pub, and she could eat three bacon cheeseburgers in a sitting. She and my boyfriend had a secret handshake, and she called him every night at seven just to talk.

Needless to say, I loathed her from the start. I'm telling you this because I do believe it was the most severe case of "boyfriend with a hot best friend syndrome" I've ever seen, and it turned out just fine. At the end of the day, I was the girlfriend, and that was that. Frankly, I didn't want to play darts with the guy, or create a secret couples handshake. I wanted to date him, and that's what I did. Don't panic. There is a reason he's dating you and not her.

You may never come to like her (I certainly never liked Barbie), but it's important to keep your thoughts about her to yourself (and your ten closest friends), and not to nag your boyfriend about it. Don't give him some sort of her-or-me ultimatum. He will think you're being jealous and controlling, and he'll be right. As the two of you get closer, they will probably grow more distant (and perhaps she'll get a job in Switzerland!). It would be naïve to think that all close male-female friendships are purely platonic—there is usually some element of "what if" there, even if neither party ever plans to act on it. Generally, best friendships between men and women tend to die down considerably when someone gets a serious significant other. Until that glorious day, here's how to deal with her.

**Don't talk to her about your relationship.** Yes, she's a woman. And yes, chances are she is in possession of a whole wealth of information about your relationship. But she's in his camp, and no good can come of confiding in her about your man. If she broaches the subject, change it.

**Act like you want to get to know her.** You don't have to break out the Best Friends necklace, but do suggest to your boyfriend that the three of you hang out sometimes. You might learn that she's actually cool, or, even better, that under her slip dress she is covered in reptilian scales.

**Don't ask your boyfriend (or worse, her) why they never got together.** Let me lay out the possible scenarios right now, so you can save yourself hours of obsessing. She might have been interested in him and he just wasn't feeling it. In that case, who cares? Or he may have been interested in her, and she wasn't feeling it. This one might cause steam to flow from your ears, but again, who cares? All it means is that he was attracted to someone dumb enough to turn him down, and thanks to her, you've got him now. She's not going to decide that she's in love with him just because you've come along—and if she does, your man will set her straight if he's as great as you think he is. The only other possibility is that they did indeed date or fool around. Don't get any more stressed about this than you would about him dating any other girl. Once we hit semi-adulthood, we've all got a past. What matters now is that he's with you for a reason, and (as long as you manage to keep your wits about you) that's how he'll stay.

**Try to set her up with someone.** Maybe then she'll go away. And if she's anything like Barbie, you won't have any trouble finding a guy to take her off your hands. If she's already seeing someone, try to refrain from cornering him at your next party and asking "Okay, what the hell do you think of this friendship and how can we make it vanish?"

## Meet the Parents

Meeting his parents for the first time is possibly more daunting than the first date. Convincing him that you're fantastic was one thing. But convincing his mother that you can take care of her baby boy (and that you're not just in it for the family fortune) is another matter entirely. Just as wealthy men can be broken down into categories, so, too, can the couples who raised them. Before we move on to how to handle his parents, let's first explore the cast of characters with whom you are dealing.

### The Old Money WASPs

*Their story:* Met when he was a junior at Harvard, she a freshman at Radcliffe. Had their wedding at the Ritz, and joined not only their hearts but their two family fortunes, for a lifetime of (slightly cool, utterly unemotional) happiness.

*Opening line from Mom* (as she extends her bony hand to shake yours): "So nice to meet you. We've heard great things. But Winston Jr. still hasn't told us where you went to prep school."

*Uniforms:* He will most likely wear a blazer and khakis, even if it's August. She will be keeping Ann Taylor in business, with a twin set, knee-length skirt, and pearls. This is not the time to showcase your love of tie-dye or that new Betsey Johnson tutu.

*Dinner menu:* Mom hasn't worked since her last babysitting job in high school, but that certainly doesn't mean that she's been slaving over a hot stove for thirty years. In fact, she might be hard-pressed to find it without a map. Not to worry, because the cook on-staff (Mom will say, "She's more like a family member") makes a mean salmon with new potatoes, and apple cobbler for dessert. And Dad makes a strong gin and tonic (no more than two! If he forces drinks on you, slip them to the yellow Lab).

*Real estate:* Their New England home is pretty much like all others—white clapboard exterior, black shutters. The only difference is that it's about ten times the size of most, has eight bathrooms, and comfortably sleeps seventeen. We're thinking Kennedy. We're thinking compound. Oriental rugs are everywhere, as are vestiges of the family's expensive taste through the ages—busts, grandfather clocks, vintage Tiffany china. You'll know you've been accepted when you get invited to their second home, a beach house in Ogunquit or Martha's Vineyard.

*Pros and cons:* You may feel like a candidate for Best in Show, with all his mother's inquiries into exactly how well-bred you are. Give her a break. She's been plotting her little boy's future ever since she sent him off to boarding school at the age of four. They're a bit snobby and not particularly warm (except after a lot of scotch), but that might make your man appreciate your love all the more.

*Future prediction:* You've loved the name Holden ever since you read *Catcher in the Rye* in seventh grade, but kiss your baby names good-bye. Think your man's name plus "the fourth" if you want to keep the peace. You'll argue about prep school, sleepover camp, and live-in nannies, but as long as you don't make his mother feel like you disagree with her choices, expect many seaside family vacations and (someday) a lot of family heirlooms in your inherited McMansion.

## The Self-Made Millionaires

*Their story:* Neither of them grew up with any money, but through hard work (or, in some cases, dumb luck) they were able to raise their son in the lap of luxury.

*Opening line from Mom:* "I see you've noticed the Jackson Pollock in the front hall. It's an original, of course. Eight million dollars, and worth every penny."

*Uniforms:* You'll see more designer labels over the course of a weekend at their place than you would in Bryant Park during fashion week. If you tell Mom that you love her Gucci stilettos, she just might say that she has four pairs, and let you keep them.

*Dinner menu:* They will take you to the trendiest (and most expensive) restaurant in town. Dad will order a $400 bottle of wine, Mom will keep talking about the months-long waiting list. Just eat your caviar risotto in a red wine reduction like it's the best thing you've ever tasted, and try to look impressed.

*Real estate:* Penthouse apartment in the city's most expensive area. The kitchen looks like it's from *The Jetsons*—chrome surfaces and all the latest gadgets and appliances (still unused). The living room is all-white. The modern art that covers every wall is original, and probably cost a fortune.

*Pros and cons:* This couple likes money, and loves spending it as flamboyantly as possible. However, since they've made it all on their own, they can't imagine why anyone else struggles financially. Once you get to know them, you'll understand why your boyfriend thinks nothing of blowing $4,000 on one trip to the Armani store.

*Future prediction:* You might fight with your mother-in-law about her attempt to buy the kids a pony (even though she rarely spends an entire afternoon with them) or her insistence that your husband get a jet that matches his dad's, but all will be forgiven during one of your semi-regular shopping sprees together.

## The Regular Joes and Flos

*Their story:* This traditional couple met in high school, and each of them worked two jobs to keep the family afloat. They raised their kids with the belief that each generation should do a little better than the last. Through loans and scholarships, they put their boy through Georgetown and Johns Hopkins med school.

*Opening line from Mom:* "What do your folks do?"

*Uniforms:* Jeans and sneakers. Depending on the season, Mom may or may not be wearing a holiday-inspired sweatshirt covered in puffy paint and an iron-on Christmas tree/Easter bunny/turkey, etc. Try to look genuinely surprised when she tells you that she made it herself.

*Dinner menu:* Roast chicken or beef, mashed potatoes, string beans, and homemade apple pie. No drinking. The only thing they guzzle down is Sunny Delight with breakfast.

*Real estate:* A modest house in the suburbs with a two-car garage and a swing set in the backyard.

*Pros and cons:* These two are as down-to-earth as they come. They will make excellent grandparents (why do you think they kept that swing set up when all their kids are already out of college?), and provide a great model of a married couple. But you and your man will have to prove that even though you have more money than they did, you don't have your heads in the clouds (leave the Dior sunglasses at home, and mum's the word on your new live-in personal chef).

*Future prediction:* If you plan to have kids and live close to his parents, you'll always have a built-in babysitter in his mom. If you plan not to have kids, or to live far away from his parents, prepare for his mother to hate your guts. Oh well. At least you only have to see her on holidays (and every time she flies in for an unexpected visit).

## The Southerners

*Their story:* The met at a debutante ball when they were just fifteen, and their families have done business together for centuries. Old Southern money is as old and as Southern as it gets. You'll need to ladle on the charm with these two, especially Mom. She will be sweet as honey on the surface, but as protective as a bear underneath.

*Opening line from Mom:* "Oh, sugar, you're just as pretty as Scarlett O'Hara."

*Uniforms:* Mom's rocking a lot of big, blond hair, and the big gold jewelry to match. Dad will be formal, in a suit and tie.

*Dinner menu:* Savannah crab cakes, fried green tomatoes, and fried chicken, with pecan pie for dessert. Don't think for a minute that they eat like this every night. Mom's just testing you to see what kind of Southern daughter-in-law you'll make.

*Real estate:* If you're not from the South, you might think this pillar-bedecked mansion is a museum. Rent *Gone With the Wind* and study the Twelve Acres barbecue scene so you'll know exactly how to react.

*Pros and cons:* The Southern son is a rare creature. He was raised to be stoic and manly, but also to love his mama more than life itself. Luckily, this stellar treatment of women extends to you as well. His mother wants him to be happy, so unlike some others, she won't hate you right off the bat. She may even come to love you. If not, she's a good Southern lady, so at least she'll never say it out loud.

*Future prediction:* His mother will want your kids to grow up into true gentlemen and ladies. As long as you live far enough away from her and can force your little monsters to behave themselves for a week or so every few months, you'll be fine. It's no use trying to convince her of the merits of laid-back parenting, so just give her what she wants. Think of the Southern mother like quicksand: if you don't try to rage against her, you will probably survive.

## The Amicably Divorced Couple

*Their story:* Though the marriage didn't work out, they still play mixed doubles with their second spouses every other Tuesday and have Christmas dinner under the same roof. Theirs is the kind of divorce that makes you wonder if burying your feelings might be the healthiest route there is, despite your degree in psychology.

*Opening line from Mom:* "Ben's stepmom and I were just talking about how thrilled we both are to meet you! She should be here soon."

*Uniforms:* Dad arrives in an old blazer and Mom immediately laughs, "I remember giving that to you back in the mid-nineties. Sheila, don't you buy this poor guy any clothes?" Sheila, without blinking, responds, "I do, but he always likes the things you bought so much better."

*Dinner menu:* Barbecued fish and vegetables (Sheila's recipe) made by Mom, and peppermint brownies for dessert (Mom's recipe) made by Sheila.

*Real estate:* Twin estates in the same development.

*Pros and cons:* You won't have to deal with any of the usual divorce animosity. These two will sit side by side at your wedding, and fly hand in hand to visit you when your first child is born. On the flip side, their situation is extremely freaking weird.

*Future prediction:* Having been raised in such an emotionally closed-off family, it's a safe assumption that your man has no idea how to fight properly. Your first major outburst is likely to be something along the lines of "What's wrong with you people?" as he once again showcases his "no problem" attitude in the wake of a crisis. But, despite their strangeness, his parents have a lot of love to offer—and they're clearly so tied up in their own delusions that they shouldn't bother you much.

## The Enraged-to-the-Point-of-Hysteria Divorced Couple

*Their story:* They have only two things in common: their wonderful son and their fiery mutual hatred for one another.

*Opening line from Mom:* "So, have you met what's-her-name yet?"

*Uniforms:* She will be wearing a red dress. When you compliment her on it, she'll say, "Hmph. His father hates red, which is why I love it."

*Dinner menu:* Growing up, your boyfriend had to do double-dinner every night of the week, lest one of his parents should find out that he was eating with the other. You said you wanted to know what his childhood was like, so get ready. No matter what the first parent serves, eat only half.

*Real estate:* One of them (the more bitter one, probably Mom) lives in the enormous ten-bedroom house where your man grew up. The other lives in an eight-bedroom house, which he or she refers to as, "The shack I got stuck with after the divorce."

*Pros and cons:* His parents haven't presented him with the best model, so your man might not be eager to rush into marriage. Once you do persuade him, however, you won't have to worry about his mother disliking you, since all of her negativity gets channeled elsewhere.

*Future prediction:* Major milestones like your wedding and your kids' graduations will be a serious juggling act. These two can't be within a hundred yards of each other without getting into a brawl. The good news is, your children will most likely enjoy spending time with your parents more than his, so you'll always win the fight about where to go for Thanksgiving.

## The Evil Mother

*Her story:* When your man was four, she bought him a pony. When he hit sixteen, she wrapped his brand-new Mustang up in a red bow. When he turned twenty-five, she gave him the whole damn ranch. She loves her boy. But maybe a little too much. She's never liked a single female he's brought home, and she's not about to start now. Watch out.

*Opening line from Mom:* "Funny, Nick doesn't usually go for chunky blondes."

*Uniform:* Your boyfriend's favorite colors: blue and gold. His mother's outfit: blue pants with a gold knit sweater over the top. When he tells her he loves it, she'll touch her collar and say "What? This old thing?" You might get the distinct impression that she is flirting with her own son. You are correct.

*Dinner menu:* So your man called ahead to tell Mom that you're allergic to shellfish and pine nuts. It must have slipped her mind, because for dinner, she just happened to whip up lobster in pesto sauce. Say that you're still full from lunch and drink the wine only if you've corked it yourself.

*Real estate:* The impressiveness of her palatial home is eclipsed by two very eerie observations. First, her son's childhood bedroom has been kept in perfect order, right down to the third grade soccer trophies and G.I. Joe sheets. Second, the lot next door is still vacant, and she's keeping her eye on it for when he's ready to settle down.

*Pros and cons:* You know that your man was raised by a woman who treated him like gold, which is quite possibly part of what makes him such a great partner (and the reason he never did his own laundry until you came along). However, any way you slice it, this chick is scary, and wants him all to herself.

*Future prediction:* Early on, you'll have to train your man to stand up to his mother when she tries to undermine you. But it might be hard for him to see what she's up to. After all, she's been driving girls away from him since his eighth-grade dance. Always take the high road in arguments with her—even when she casts her eyes toward you at Christmas dinner and tells your kids, "Sometimes you can't stop your children from making huge mistakes." Just remember, she may have given birth to him, but you're wearing the ring.

## The I'llBeYourBestFriend Mother

*Her story:* Maybe she just never had enough friends in high school, or perhaps she always wanted a daughter of her own. Whatever the reason, this mom has been waiting for the day when her son would bring home the ultimate prize—a playmate for her.

*Opening line from Mom* (to her son, as she links arms with you): "You take the bags upstairs, sweetheart. We need to have some girl talk."

*Uniform:* Trendy, twenty-something-wear from Theory, DKNY, and Banana Republic. Don't be surprised if some of the items in her collection are eerily similar to the ones in yours.

*Dinner menu:* Your favorites, of course. She e-mailed your boyfriend to find out what your fantasy meal would be.

*Real estate:* A seven-bedroom house complete with swimming pool, arcade, bowling alley, and movie theater. What, you think you're the first one of her son's peers she's tried to impress? Don't flatter yourself. This has been going on since he was in grade school.

*Pros and cons:* There's something disconcerting about a mother-in-law who wants to be your best friend. But hey, at least she's not the evil mom.

*Future prediction:* She will try to get you to confide in her about your marital problems. After she's spilled the beans about the fact that you wanted emerald-cut, not round, and that you would have preferred Florence to Rome as a honeymoon destination, *and* that you loved that apartment downtown that he thought was too artsy, you'll finally get it, and learn to keep her out of your relationship. Which is a good skill to master before the grandchildren come along.

## Visiting His Parents

There is a whole set of rules for how you should behave in front of your man's parents if you want them to vote for you as their future daughter-in-law. In New England, where I'm from, we call this Conn-etiquette. It involves being yourself—only more reserved, more polite, and more refined. Here are the Do's and Don'ts for the first weekend at their place.

**The Don'ts:**

- **Don't arrive empty-handed.** My great-grandmother had a saying: "Never arrive on someone's doorstep unless one of your arms is longer than the other." Despite the creepy imagery this conjured up for me when I was a kid, she just meant bring something along when you visit people. If your man's parents are hosting you for the weekend, give them a token of your thanks, such as a nice bottle of wine, homemade bread, or flowers. Nothing too excessive, just a simple means of showing them what a thoughtful, nurturing gal you are.
- **Don't dress provocatively.** If you tend to wear tops that are so low-cut they cause fender-benders, or skirts that look like they came from the wardrobe closet of an Aerosmith video shoot, stock up on turtlenecks, cardigans, and pants before you meet his parents. Your man may love your cleavage, or the fact that your legs just won't quit, but his mother will love you all the more if you keep yourself covered.
- **Don't act enamored of their wealth.** Inwardly, you may be screaming about the double *Sound of Music* staircase in their front hall, and the Degas sculpture garden out back. But don't act too impressed by their digs, or

they'll think you're not accustomed to (and therefore not worthy of) their lifestyle. It's okay to compliment them once in a general way. Simply say "You have a beautiful home," and leave it at that.

- **Don't drink too much.** Everyone tends to drink a little more when they're nervous or uncomfortable, but absolutely, positively no good can come of getting wasted in front of your boyfriend's parents. If they try to force it on you, make him drink your port when no one's looking. Better their own son singing "Margaritaville" with a lampshade on his head after dinner than you.

- **Don't make fun of/fight with your man.** Since your boyfriend is pretty much the only thing you have in common, it makes sense that you and his parents might start teasing him. This is a trap, even if they don't mean for it to be. Once I was in the car with my ex-boyfriend's father. When he took a wrong turn and apologized repeatedly, I unwisely made a crack about the fact that it was no big deal since I was used to driving with his son, who couldn't find his way out of a paper bag. My ex's dad turned serious and said, "Actually, I think Joe's quite good at reading maps. I taught him myself." Remember that his parents aren't his buddies—they have known him since before he was born, and they want him to find a woman who thinks he's just as perfect as they do. This same reasoning explains why you should never, ever fight with him in their presence.

- **Don't swear.** Even if they do it, you must not swear. They are in their own home and have nothing to prove. You are a visitor and need to be on your best behavior.

- **Don't say anything disparaging about your own family.** Remember the first date / job interview analogy in chapter 3? Well, that goes double for when you're with his parents. Don't give them anything to worry about when it comes to you and your upbringing. Parents, especially wealthy ones, are very concerned with the breeding of their future daughters-in-law. Saying something like "It's so great seeing a family sit around the table all together like this—we only do that when my dad gets time off for good behavior at Christmas" will not win you any points.

- **Don't sleep in the same room with your man unless you are engaged.** Even if you live together, even if they say it's fine—don't do it. Insist on sleeping in different rooms. If you can't imagine why this is necessary, close your eyes and think about giving birth to a baby boy someday, watching him go off to nursery school, and his first day of second grade. Imagine helping him pack up his room for college, and sending him care packages full of his favorite baked goods and taped cable shows once he gets there. Then imagine having him come back home to spoon some chick in his childhood bed while you lie in the room next door, unable to sleep. Kind of shatters the image, doesn't it? You'll have plenty of time to sleep together later. When you're at his parents' house, hit one of the seven guest rooms.

- **Don't touch your boyfriend in a flirtatious manner.** The absolute maximum you can do is hold his hand. There are a lot of ways to show his parents that you're serious about each other. Shoving your tongue down their son's throat in front of them is not one of them.

- **Don't indulge in too much we-speak.** Serious couples tend to meld into one unit called "we" after a while. You invite your girlfriend out for Sunday brunch, and she says, "We'd love to." You ask your coworker if she wants to grab an ice cream sundae after a stressful day at the office, and she says, "We're trying to cut back on our sugar intake." We-speak is annoying, but your friends tolerate it. However, your boyfriend's parents are another story. To them, "we" means the two of them and their son. While it's perfectly fine, and in fact very good, to talk about things you and your man have done together (great restaurants you've been to, plays you've seen, trips you've gone on), it's not a good idea to inform them about your collective we-beliefs, especially if they contradict the beliefs of the *other* we, such as "No thanks. We can't stand Brussels sprouts" or "Would you mind changing the channel? We never watch Fox News."

- **Don't talk on your cell phone.** Sure, at home you need to catch up with your eight closest girlfriends every day. But when you're visiting your boyfriend's parents, it's insanely rude to take a call every two seconds. Turn your phone off altogether if you can handle it. If you're a total junkie, limit yourself to one five-minute call a day, and make sure you whisper, "Oh, I've got to take this. It's my mom," before you answer the phone (hey, I didn't say you couldn't lie).

The Do's:

- **Do research Mom and Dad ahead of time.** A lot of awkwardness can be avoided if you gather information about his parents in advance. Once again, the powers of Google can come in handy (but don't tell your boyfriend you're doing that—it will creep him out). You can also just ask him flat out if there are any topics that you should avoid, or if there's anything his parents would love to talk about. If you know his mother has a passion for Victorian literature, then you can casually drop your love of *Villette* into the dinner conversation (even if you just read it for the first time on the eight-hour drive to their house).
- **Do say thank you. A lot.** No mother ever disliked her son's girlfriend because she was too grateful. Make sure to mind your manners and be gracious.
- **Do address them by their full names.** Calling his parents "Mr. and Mrs. Jones" shows that you're respectful. If they tell you to call them by their first names, by all means do. But don't assume that you should right off the bat.
- **Do eat everything on your plate and compliment his mother on her cooking, even if it's awful.** There is a delicate balance being struck between you and your

boyfriend's mother. It's a passing of the nurture torch, at least in her eyes, so she wants to know that you will be able to take good care of her son. This means feeding him (even if you eat takeout every night), clothing him (even if he was decked out in Prada long before you came along), and caring for him (even if you've screamed "Pick up your own damn clothes! I'm not your mother!" more times than you'd care to remember). However, although she is genetically programmed to want these things from you, she does not want you to be better at them than she is. Which is why you've got to make her feel like Martha Stewart. Ask for seconds, and if the spirit moves you, ask for her recipes—even if you're planning to use the note cards for scrap paper when you get home.

- **Do offer to help.** Every family is different. Some will be delighted if you offer to pitch in, some won't hear of it, and some have a full staff to make sure that you (and they) never have to lift a finger in the first place. Whatever the case, it's nice to at least offer to set the table, help prepare dinner, or wash the dishes. They will probably say no, but the gesture will make you look good.
- **Do ask about your boyfriend's childhood.** Look through old scrapbooks and photo albums with his mom, drive around his hometown and let his dad point out the elementary school and the baseball field, encourage them to tell stories. This will put them at ease, show them that you're serious about their son, and provide you with ample ammunition to make fun of him

once you're back at home. It's important to let his parents (especially his mother) know that you have no intention of stealing him away, but rather that you want to become a part of their already-established family.

- **Do wear pajamas that make you look like you're Amish, even if you usually sleep naked.** Why tempt fate? Break out that flannel nightgown that your grandmother gave you last Christmas. Your boyfriend has seen you naked. You know it, he knows it, and his parents know it. But none of you should be reminded of that fact in his childhood home.
- **Do take part in their rituals.** If his mama goes to eight o'clock Mass on Sunday morning, so do you when you're sleeping under her roof (even if you're not religious). If his family likes nothing better than breakfast at dawn, you'll have to forgo your own sleeping-until-noon routine just this once. Be respectful and show them that you know how to go with the flow. A weekend at his parents' house is not a vacation—it's a chance to prove that you're the daughter-in-law they've always wanted.
- **Do be yourself.** If all of these do's and don'ts leave you feeling like you'll have to play a part the whole time you're visiting his parents, relax. Most of these guidelines are just good common sense (I mean, come on, swearing in front of his mother and sleeping in your thong? You weren't planning to do those things anyway). Ultimately, his parents will fall in love with you for the same reason he did—because you're fabulous.

## SECRET WEAPON: Tricia Sweeney's Recipes

Despite your greatest efforts, some mothers are nearly impossible to win over. They don't like your hair, they don't like your job, they don't like the fact that you allow their son to subsist on a steady diet of lo mein and Dr Pepper. These women require the big guns. They require homemade baked goods.

Perhaps you've heard of Mrs. Fields or Betty Crocker, but if you've never heard of Tricia Sweeney, then you don't know the reigning queen of American baking. I grew up next door to Mrs. Sweeney (her daughter Kate was one of my best friends), and her kitchen was always a magical place full of cookies and pies, all baked from scratch. I asked her to share some of her best recipes with me for this section, and tried baking them myself—the results are astounding.

You may not be at all domestic, but it behooves you to follow these recipes and bring one or more of these treats along the next time you visit your man's mother. Act like it's no big thing when she takes that first bite of heaven. It will be smooth sailing between you from then on out.

### Jam Squares

These yummy bars never stay around for very long in Mrs. Sweeney's kitchen. They are super-easy to make, and travel well (provided you don't eat all of them in the car before you reach your mother-in-law's house).

½ cup sugar
½ cup shortening

1 egg
½ teaspoon almond extract
1 ½ cups all-purpose flour
½ teaspoon salt
½ teaspoon baking powder
¾ cup jam, any flavor (I think raspberry works best)

Preheat oven to 400 degrees Fahrenheit. Grease and flour an 8-by-8-inch baking pan.

In a medium size mixing bowl, blend the sugar, shortening, egg, and almond extract. Set aside.

In a smaller bowl, combine the flour, salt, and baking powder. Then add the dry ingredients to the shortening mixture and blend well.

Spread half of the dough in the 8-by-8-inch pan. Cover with the jam.

Roll the remaining dough between two sheets of waxed paper cut to the size of the pan. Peel off one sheet, and place the exposed dough on top of the jam. Gently peel off the remaining waxed paper.

Bake for 25 to 30 minutes, until lightly browned.

## Scones

Perfect for a heart-to-heart with his mom during one of those long weekend visits when he is still snoring away in his childhood bed at noon and you need an icebreaker. You can add a little orange zest if you like. Serve with good butter and hot tea.

1 ½ cup raisins
1 tablespoon water
½ cup butter (1 stick)
2 cups all-purpose flour
3 tablespoons sugar
½ teaspoon salt
4 teaspoons baking powder
1 cup whole milk

Preheat oven to 450 degrees Fahrenheit. Lightly grease a large cookie sheet.

Moisten the raisins with the water. Set aside.

In a large mixing bowl, cut the butter into the flour and mix until crumbly. Add the sugar, salt, and baking powder and stir well. Add the raisins. Slowly pour the milk in until dough forms (you may not need the whole cup).

Mix lightly, forming the dough into a ball. (Be careful not to overmix!)

Place the dough on a lightly floured countertop, and gently press it flat until it's about an inch thick. Then cut it into 1½- to 2-inch squares, and place the squares on the cookie sheet.

Bake for 11 to 12 minutes, being careful not to let the bottoms burn. Once they are cooked, place them on a cooling rack.

## White Chocolate Raspberry Swirl Cheesecake

This is the biggest of all the big guns. A truly magnificent dessert. It's more difficult to make than the others, but it's worth it. When my friend Noreen graduated from high school, the one present she wanted was Mrs. Sweeney's cheesecake. If your man's mother invites you to a dinner party, convince her to let you bring dessert, and bake this masterpiece. She may just propose to you herself.

28 vanilla wafers
1 1/4 cup sliced almonds (toasted)
3 tablespoons butter, melted
2 tablespoons sugar
12 ounces frozen raspberries, thawed
4 teaspoons cornstarch
6 ounces white chocolate
4 (8-ounce) packages of cream cheese
3/4 cup sugar
4 large eggs
1/2 teaspoon almond extract
2 teaspoons Chambord
1/2 cup heavy cream
1/4 cup confectioner's sugar
fresh raspberries

Preheat oven to 450 degrees Fahrenheit.

In a food processor or blender, mix the vanilla wafers and 1/4 cup of the almonds until they form fine crumbs. Combine the wafer mixture with the 2 tablespoons sugar and butter. Press it to the bottom of a 9-inch springform pan, and set aside.

Puree the frozen raspberries in a food processor or blender. Press the pureed fruit through a fine sieve into a 2-quart saucepan. Stir the cornstarch into the raspberries and cook over medium heat, stirring constantly until the mixture thickens and boils. Allow to boil for 1 minute, then remove the pan from the heat and let cool.

Melt the white chocolate.

In a large bowl, with mixer at low speed, beat cream cheese and 3/4 cup sugar just until smooth. Add the melted white chocolate, eggs, and almond extract. Beat until blended.

Place 1 cup of the cream cheese mixture in a small bowl, and reserve 2 tablespoons of the raspberry mixture for later. Stir the Chambord and the remaining raspberry mixture into the single cup of cream cheese mixture.

Pour half of the plain cream cheese mixture into the pan, and spread. Next, drop half of the raspberry/cream cheese mixture by spoonfuls on top. With a knife, gently swirl the two together. Repeat this process to form another marbleized layer.

Bake for 10 minutes. Reduce heat to 250 degrees Fahrenheit, and bake for another 30 to 35 minutes, until the center of the cake is just barely firm. Cool in pan on a rack. Cover and refrigerate for at least 4 hours.

Remove from pan. Spread sides of cake with reserved raspberry puree, and press toasted almonds over it.

When you're ready to serve, whip the cream until stiff (sweeten with confectioner's sugar to taste) and put a dollop on each slice. Garnish with fresh raspberries.

## Top Ten Reasons to Stay in His Mother's Good Graces Or, If You Can't Beat Her, Join Her

Remember in fifth grade, when you were two feet taller than all the males in your class, and your teacher said that girls just mature faster than boys? Well, news flash: nowhere is that more true than in the world of dating and marriage. According to Aristotle, "The appropriate age for marriage is around eighteen for girls and thirty-seven for men."

So who are men devoting their hearts to before they finally give into matrimony? It doesn't matter if they were shipped off to boarding school, left in the care of a nanny named Helga, or raised by wolves—all men are mama's boys. My recommendation: put this book down right now, and call his mother to see if you can take her to lunch (don't worry, she'll pay). If she doesn't like you, the only ring you'll be receiving is the one your telephone emits when he calls to say he can't see you anymore. Don't believe me? Here are some quotes on the topic from nine famous men and one very wise woman. (*Warning:* As with swimming, best to wait a half hour after eating before you read this list.)

1. "All that I am, or hope to be, I owe to my angel mother."
   —*Abraham Lincoln*

2. "There never was a woman like her. She was gentle as a dove and brave as a lioness. The memory of my mother and her teachings were, after all, the only capital I had to start life with, and on that capital I have made my way."
   —*Andrew Jackson*

3. "My mother was the most beautiful woman I ever saw. I attribute all my success in life to the moral, intellectual and physical education I received from her."
   —*George Washington*

4. "If I have done anything in life worth attention, I feel sure that I inherited the disposition from my mother."
   —*Booker T. Washington*

5. "You're the best mom in the whole, wide world!"
   —*Beaver Cleaver*

6. "God could not be everywhere, and therefore he made mothers."
   —*Rudyard Kipling*

7. "All women become like their mothers. That is their tragedy. No man does. That's his."
   —*Oscar Wilde*

8. "The heart of a mother is a deep abyss at the bottom of which you will always find forgiveness."
   —*Balzac*

9. "Men are what their mothers made them."
   —*Ralph Waldo Emerson*

10. "Happy is the son whose faith in his mother remains unchallenged."
    —*Louisa May Alcott*

## Conn-etiquette 101

If you're lucky, his parents are wonderful and love you for who you are. Or perhaps they live in some faraway land, and you only have to see them at Christmas. Either way. For the rest of us, there are numerous social occasions that we will have to endure with our boyfriend and his parents throughout the course of a year. How you act at their house during dinner is one thing. But the way you conduct yourself in public around their extended group of family and friends—at weddings, bar mitzvahs, holiday parties, and more—might just make the difference between his parents' loving you, and his parents' begging him to leave you. The good news is that in large part, you can convince his parents that you are The One just by having impeccable manners.

I have always been obsessed with the rules of etiquette and the fairy godmother of those rules, Miss Manners. In my opinion, owning a copy of *Miss Manners' Guide for the Turn of the Millennium* is as essential as owning a complete works of Shakespeare, or the Bible. However, I do take issue with something the Divine Miss M says about the wealthy in the introduction to that book:

> It is astonishing to Miss Manners that so many people presume that the gentle art of manners is based on a preoccupation with money . . . She doesn't know which offends her more—people who seek to demonstrate their genuineness by eschewing manners or those who are scrambling to learn them to serve their social ambitions. They all end up rude. The truth is that there is very little relationship between

> manners and money. Certainly, Miss Manners has never noticed any preponderance of politeness on the part of the rich.

It is true that money can't buy manners. However, if you are trying to find and marry the right kind of rich man—one who has money and uses it to better his life—then etiquette will be an essential part of impressing his family and making him yours. This next section should provide a cheat sheet to doing just that.

## Thank-You Notes

Thank-you notes are key, and show his parents that you're one classy lady. The money you'll spend on the stamp will be well worth it when his mother suggests that he give you his great-grandmother's diamond. It's always a good idea to send his parents a thank-you note after an overnight visit to their house, or when they've given you a gift (even if it was an ugly lime-green Lilly Pulitzer cardigan). In the age of e-mail, actual notes (with actual stamps on them) might seem like a pain. Send them anyway. I once dashed off a thank-you note to an ex-boyfriend's parents, and after a week, my own parents got a note from his mother in the mail. It read:

> *Dear Mr. and Mrs. Sullivan,*
>
> *My husband and I recently had the great pleasure of hosting Courtney for the weekend. She is a lovely young lady and we truly enjoyed her company. However, neither of us could believe it when we received a thank-you note in the mail from*

*her a few days later. I didn't know that young people even knew how to send those anymore! You have raised a wonderful daughter, and we are thrilled to have her in our lives.*

*Sincerely,*
*Mrs. Unlike-My-Son-I-Know-a-Good-Thing-When-I-See-It*

Yes, my mother saved that note.

The few minutes it takes to write a card might mean a lifetime of wedded bliss—with your mother-in-law. Just make sure to send it no more than a couple of days after you see them (or after you receive the lime green cardigan), address them by their full names (unless they've instructed you to call them something else), make at least one reference to something pleasant you did together, and one reference to the next time you'll see them (even if it's just "looking forward to seeing you again soon"). If the only stationery you own has commemorative Jerry Garcia artwork on the front, probably best to shell out the three bucks for a blank card with a floral print or tasteful black-and-white photograph on the cover. Follow the example below, and do this *every* time you visit her, even after you're married, because some mothers-in-law are all too delighted to complain about you to their sons (not yours, of course, but still better to be safe than sorry).

*June 5, 2006*
*Dear Mr. and Mrs. Jones,*

*It was so nice to finally meet you both in person this past weekend. Thank you for your hospitality. I've been telling everyone about the amazing dinner we had at Chez Snooty—*

*the foie gras was fantastic, and I'm still laughing over your hilarious story about snorkeling in St. Tropez! Looking forward to seeing you at Mitzy's wedding in August.*

*All Best,*
*Courtney*

## Going Out with His Parents

Just because you're now in a happy and healthy relationship doesn't mean that you get to avoid the awkwardness of first dates—you still have to deal with going out with his parents and other family members. The first dinner with them in a restaurant is crucial. Eating at their house is one thing, but being out in public with them is quite another. It's your chance to show them how sophisticated you are, and it's potentially your foray into more intimate family affairs like weddings and birthday parties (don't stress—I'll cover the best way to handle those in a minute). Some things to bear in mind:

**Turn off your cell phone.** Unless you are an Emergency Room doctor on-call, your cell phone should never ring when you're in a restaurant. It's horribly rude to your dinner companions and other patrons. Don't risk it. Make sure your phone is switched off before you sit down.

**Passing etiquette.** If you want to get technical, remember that when the person beside you asks you to pass the salt, you should pick it up and place it directly on the table in front of him, *not* put it straight into his hands. Always pass to the right.

**Which dinnerware is yours?** If you are with several people at a round table, the glasses to your right and the bread plate to your left are the ones you should use. One way to remember when you are at the table: subtly make two "OK" signs with your hands. You'll notice the left hand makes a "b" (for bread), and the right hand makes a "d" (for drink).

**Keep up with the crowd.** You may eat like a goldfish when you're on your own—one flake of food every hour or so—but when you're out with your man's family, it's important to eat and drink at the speed they establish. There's nothing worse than staring down an empty plate while they're still cutting their first bites of filet mignon, or forcing them to wait for you to finish your salad before they can start their entrées.

**Take part in the conversation.** Engage his family members in discussion topics other than yourself. Talk about politics, art, film, and books you've read recently. It's a good idea to block off several hours the day of the dinner to read the *New York Times* cover-to-cover. That way you'll be sure to have something to talk about other than your job and what city you were born in. Remember that though they do want to get to know you, you can make yourself stand out from the pack by having interesting and insightful things to say.

**Let them pay.** It may feel a bit awkward to let them pay for your fifty-dollar plate of confit duck, but as on dates, resist the urge to reach for your wallet. If your man's parents or other relatives have invited you to dine out, then they fully expect to pay for you. Thinking otherwise makes you look rude. Just be sure to send them a thank-you card (yes, even just for dinner) as soon as you get home.

## Deciphering Dress Codes

Dress codes, especially at events hosted by the very wealthy, are quite frankly getting out of hand. In the past three months alone, friends have received invitations instructing them to wear "Summer Chic," "Miami Beach Casual," "Midnight Formalwear," and "Mardi Gras Style" to various events. It's stressful business, particularly when you're attending formal events with your man and his family. How can you decode the codes so that you don't end up arriving to his parents' party wearing a sarong and a fruit basket while everyone else is in capri pants and tanks? Read on.

- **Black tie.** For formal events that take place during the evening hours. Traditionally means sleeved dinner dresses with long narrow skirts, but you can get away with something a little shorter (just make sure it's knee-length and in a dark color).
- **White tie.** More formal than a black tie affair, wear a solid-color ball gown with a wide skirt. No leather bags or shoes, and no daytime accessories (according to Miss Manners, these spoil the effect). Evening gloves should be white kid or doeskin (even if you were a founding member of your campus PETA group), and all jewelry should be tucked inside. Note from Miss Manners: "Ladies wear gloves when they are guests. They need not remove gloves for shaking hands or dancing, but if

a lady so much as touches anything to eat or drink with a glove on, warts will grow all over the hand underneath." Consider yourself warned.

- **Semiformal.** For a cocktail party, or any other event that specifies semiformal attire, break out your little black dress and heels. Once again, leave those daytime accessories at home, and wear some nice (but subtle) jewelry.
- **Dress optional (or black tie optional).** This is when a host wants to have a black tie affair, but doesn't want guests to feel pressured into dressing too formally if they don't want to. Follow the rules for black tie, no matter what. Let some other girl wear her cutest Juicy Couture sweat suit in a sea of floor-length gowns.
- **For weddings.** Never wear black or white, no matter what. If it's a formal wedding, wear a long afternoon dress (hat and gloves optional) during the day, or an evening gown at night. For an informal wedding, more casual dresses are okay. If you have some need to break out the floral prints, now's the time to do it.

## Wedding and Shower Gifts

Depending on how close you live to his family, as your relationship progresses you will probably be called upon to attend many social functions with them. Giving a gift with your guy can be nerve-wracking, especially if it's for one of his relatives or family friends, because let's face it—even in this day and age, the burden's going to fall on you, not him, if the gift isn't a hit. Luckily, every engaged couple's registry can be accessed right from home at www.theknot.com.

For showers, which are often themed, bring a small household gift from the registry that goes along with the theme (e.g., glasses and a bottle of wine if it's a kitchen theme). For wedding gifts, a more substantial (read: expensive) gift from the registry is required. You may have heard that you have one year from the wedding date to deliver a present—don't believe everything you hear. It's best to order a gift far in advance, making sure that it's delivered to the bride and groom on or before the wedding day (do not, under any circumstances, bring it to the wedding). And yes, even if you do not plan on attending the wedding, you must send a gift.

## Baby Presents

These days even babies have registries. Before a baby shower, the godmother (or whoever is throwing the event) will likely let you know where the mother-to-be has registered. If not, appropriate traditional gifts include clothing, nice baby blankets, or anything from Tiffany's baby line.

Oftentimes, couples will have religious ceremonies for newborns—the christening in Christian families, or the briss in the Jewish faith. This does indeed call for a second gift, even if you've already shelled out a hundred and sixty bucks for a sterling silver rattle. A sweet idea for a baby girl who is born to someone very close (i.e., your boyfriend's sibling) is a single pearl on a gold chain. For each milestone through the next eighteen years—birthdays, holidays, graduations—you can provide her with another pearl, until the necklace is complete. I like this as a gift for a family member of your (very) serious boyfriend or fiancé (don't do this if you've only known his family for a year or less), because it sends the message that you intend to be around for a while.

And one last thing—if the baby has older siblings, you can score major brownie points with the parents if you bring along Big Brother or Big Sister presents, too.

### Funerals

Perhaps it's sick of me to say it, but you know you've arrived as a fixture when your man invites you to a family funeral. This is a vital time to be on your best behavior. Proper funeral attire is black for the family and subdued dark colors for friends. In a funeral line, it is best to say "I'm so sorry" and keep moving. No other remarks are necessary. If the death is that of a close relative, it is customary to send flowers to the funeral home, bring food to the grieving, and ask members of the relative's immediate family if there is anything they'd like you to do—babysitting, errands, or whatever it might be. If the death is that of your boyfriend's more distant relative, send a condolence letter on white stationery.

## Introducing Your Family to His

I will never forget the night I introduced my warm, laid-back parents to my first serious boyfriend's family. They were uptight, never hugged one another, and (naturally) they were insanely rich. At dinnertime, my family gathers (with *Enter-*

*tainment Tonight* playing in the background) to talk about the people we know and love—where my cousin is going for his honeymoon, how my sister is doing in school, a funny joke that my uncle called to tell my dad earlier in the day. This guy's family rarely ate together, and when they did, they talked about world affairs or read the paper. Not that either way is the *right* way, but needless to say, our parents didn't exactly get along like a house on fire. Still, we kept dating for two more years. If your families are likely to be as in love as the two of you, congratulations! If not, follow these guidelines for a smooth introduction:

**Make your boyfriend your ally.** If you're at the point where family introductions are necessary, then you should be long past the point where you feel the need to impress your boyfriend. Tell him about your hesitations, and develop a game plan together. You'll be a lot more relaxed if you know you have an ally at the table.

**Meet in a neutral location.** Skip the long and awkward meeting at one couple's home. Instead, suggest that the six of you go out for brunch or dinner and make sure that you pick the restaurant. That way, no one has home-court advantage, and the meeting will naturally come to an end after an hour or two. If they get along, there will be plenty of time for home visits in the future. If they don't, a meal in a restaurant makes for a quick escape.

**Establish common ground topics ahead of time.** Brainstorm with your boyfriend to come up with at least six or eight general topics on which you know your parents can agree (restaurants both sets love, grandchildren they can't stop talking about, a favorite museum or gallery). When the conversation turns to something that they clearly will not agree on, you can interject and change to a safer subject.

**Stay loyal to the people who raised you.** One of life's most unpleasant predicaments arises when you are in the presence of two women who can't get along, and one of them is your mom, the other your future mother-in-law. On the one hand, you want your future mother-in-law to like you. On the other hand, your mother gave birth to you, raised you, and put you through college. She wins. Unless Mom is advocating drowning kittens, be on her side. Your mother-in-law should respect you all the more for your loyalty. If she doesn't, you and your mom have something new to gossip about.

**Don't expect perfection.** The odds are your parents and his will not be immediate best friends. Don't worry. They're only meeting because of their shared love of their children, not to find the perfect pals with whom to play tennis on Sundays. While you're all together, remember to breathe, relax, and remind yourself—it will be over soon.

## Dating 911

So his friends love you, his mother adores you, and your one-year anniversary is just a distant memory. Congrats! Now you can kick back and live happily ever after.

Ha. Just kidding.

In a perfect world, that would be all you'd need to learn—how to find a man, how to hook him, and how to reel him in. But as any woman who has ever been in a relationship knows, dating is anything but perfect. Here are some of the more common disasters we face in Dateland, and advice for how to get through them alive.

## If He Cheats on You

Cheating is never a good sign. There's a reason why Hallmark doesn't make greeting cards that say "Congratulations! You cheated!" But the way in which the infidelity happened, and the circumstances surrounding it, can usually help to determine whether your relationship can survive. Here are the key elements to weigh if you find out that your man has strayed.

- **Has he done it more than once?** One drunken kiss with a stranger in a coat closet may not be the best thing in the world, but it may not be the worst. We all make mistakes. However, an actual affair is a different matter—if he's been carrying on a relationship with another woman, or has repeatedly been with one or more people while he's been with you, send him packing.
- **Has he done it in the past?** Some people are addicted to cheating. My friend Greg has cheated on every woman he's ever been with. When he met Melanie, a beautiful, funny architect who worked in his firm, he was smitten from the start: "I'm never cheating again," he told me. A year later they were engaged—and that's when Greg met Emily. I don't necessarily believe in the whole "once

a cheater, always a cheater" philosophy, but three or four or five times a cheater? If the guy's made a habit of it his whole life, don't fool yourself into thinking you can change him now.

- **How far did it go?** It's up to you to determine what sort of infidelity you will and will not accept. But if he's been sleeping with someone else—even if it happened only once, even if he knows it was a huge mistake—I urge you to end your relationship. By having sex with another woman, he has sent a very strong message about how much he respects you. Which is to say, not very much. And on top of that, he's put your health at risk to satisfy his own curiosity. You deserve better than that and you know it.

- **How did you find out about it?** If he comes clean about what he's done pretty quickly after it's happened, that's one thing. It shows that he knows it's important to be honest with you, that he's taking responsibility for what occurred, and that he probably feels pretty damn bad. But if you have to hear it from someone else, or if he suddenly grows a conscience and springs a "Honey, remember that business trip to Seattle I took two years ago?" on you, that's a bad sign. The worst part of cheating, of course, is not usually the act that took place—it's the sense of betrayal that you feel upon finding out. Just by cheating, he has lied to you. But if he doesn't tell you about it right away, he shows that he's capable of lying in more ways than one.

- **Does he swear that it will never happen again?** And do you believe him? Love makes us do strange—some might say psychotic—things. Like forgive someone who is totally undeserving of our forgiveness. If you find out he cheated and has no intention of stopping (or if he says it's over but the mysterious incoming calls on his cell phone say otherwise), tell him to shove it.
- **Do you really want to forgive him? Or do you just want to punish him a little while longer before breaking up?** The most important question to ask yourself is whether you want to be with him anymore in light of what's happened. You know yourself better than anyone else does. Can you forgive an indiscretion of this kind? Will you be able to trust him again? Of course, sometimes it takes a little bit of time to figure out, but if a few months have gone by and you're still thinking about what he did every day, it might be time to consider leaving. I once had a roommate whose boyfriend of seven years cheated on her. She told herself (and me, and anyone else who would listen) that it didn't mean anything—she had forgiven him, and they were moving on. Then one day she casually announced to me over breakfast that she had placed an ad on the Web site Craigslist asking random Manhattan women to help her trap her man in the act. These strangers (she got fifty replies in the first hour after she posted the message) agreed to try to seduce her boyfriend in his favorite after-work hangout, then report back to my roommate on whether or not he went home with them.

"It's no big deal," she told me. "This is just the only way I can think of to know for sure." Whoa there, cowgirl. If you're considering resorting to such measures, your trust in him is nonexistent. Better to get off the horse now than to ride it straight into Crazyland.

## If You Cheat on Him

The only reason *not* to have a zero tolerance policy when men cheat is that sometimes we slip up and do it, too. You may think you would never ever cheat—until you do. Unfortunately, all of the above has to be true for you as well if you've cheated and you want forgiveness—you've got to be honest, you've got to say you're going to stop (and mean it), and if you find yourself starting to go down that path, you've got to make sure it doesn't go too far. A few other things:

**Talkin' with the (wo)man in the mirror.** When someone cheats on you, the one word that crosses your mind about eight hundred times a day is *Why. Why did he do it? Why did he hurt me? Why don't I believe that it won't happen again?* And so on. When you're the cheater, you should be asking yourself the very same questions. Did you cheat because you wanted to get even? To make him jealous? Because your ex has reappeared and you've suddenly realized that you still have feelings for him? Because you were drunk and the other guy had a six-pack that could not be ignored? Figuring out why you did it, instead of telling yourself that it was just a stupid mistake, will help you know how to proceed.

**To tell or not to tell.** It pains me to say this knowing that my future husband and my mother will read it, but I have to confess. I cheated once. It wasn't a *huge* indiscretion—I had had about six gin and tonics at a party, my boyfriend of three years was living in London, and I missed him. I started chatting with some guy, and ended up kissing him on the dance floor. That same night, at that same apartment, a close friend of mine also cheated on her long-distance boyfriend (it was quite a party, folks). The next morning, the first thing I did was call my friend Lauren in Ithaca. Should I tell my boyfriend? And if so, how? My overwhelming feeling was that I should tell him, and so I did, as soon as I'd hung up with Lauren. When I broke the news, there was a long pause, and then he said, "Why are you telling me this?" I'd thought I was doing it to be honest, but at that moment I realized that perhaps in part, I'd told him so that I could stop feeling like the most wicked person on earth, and instead feel a teeny tiny bit noble. Yes, I'd messed up big-time. But at least I'd been honest about it. He was the kindest and most forgiving man I've ever known, let alone dated. He said he needed some time to think about it, thought about it for an hour, and then called me back and said that as long as I could swear that it wouldn't happen again, we could move on as if nothing had occurred. I swore, and we did just that. My friend, on the other hand, never told her boyfriend about that night—it was a onetime thing, she said, a fluke. Why stress her boyfriend out? Of course, just as I was trying to make myself feel better by telling, she was doing the same by not telling. You have to judge the situation for yourself and act in his best interest, not your own. If it was one kiss and it will never be repeated, would your man even want to know? Would you want him to tell you if he kissed some stranger? If the cheating is more intense than that—if you've slept with someone, or entered into an actual relationship with him—you must tell your boyfriend if you want your bond to survive.

**You'll have to pay the price.** My friend and I were both fortunate. After our night of gin-induced double damage, we both managed to keep our boyfriends and move on with our relationships. But you might not be so lucky. A lot of guys just flat-out cannot handle knowing that their girlfriends have been with someone else. If he leaves because of what you did, even if you feel that it was just a blip on the radar screen, you'll have to accept his decision. And you'll have to admit that the relationship ended because you violated his trust. If you hate the way that feels, take it as a learning experience and vow to never cheat again. But at the same time . . .

**Forgive yourself.** Regardless of whether or not he can get over what you did, *you* absolutely must. After the aforementioned drunken debauchery, I felt so guilty that I overcompensated in every way imaginable—I made sure my boyfriend knew where I was at all times, I limited myself to two drinks every night I went out, I apologized to him way more than he wanted or needed to be apologized to. I was raised Catholic, so I guess in a way, I was doing penance. One incident (or maybe even a few) doesn't make you a bad person or a horrible partner. It may have been a stupid decision, but now all you can do is move on and make better choices next time.

**If you can't stop doing it.** Greg is not my only friend with a freakish propensity for cheating. Many women I know can't stop fooling around, no matter how much they love their boyfriends (or, in some cases, their husbands—oy). If you're in this category, it's probably a good idea to speak to a therapist about why you can't stay faithful. It could be that you're afraid of making a deep commitment, or that you don't trust your partner. Whatever the reason, repeated behavior keeps being repeated until you figure out how to stop it.

## If You Fight So Much, Your Matches Should Be Broadcast on Pay-Per-View

My first serious boyfriend and I fought so much that we actually invented a Richter scale to measure the severity of each fight. We'd have a whopper over the phone, I'd hang up on him, then an hour later he'd call and say, "Five on the Richter scale." Or we'd scream at each other in a restaurant until he stormed out, leaving me there to pay the check. But later, he'd call me and say, "Sorry. That was definitely a nine." Despite all the drama (or because of it?) we were together for three tumultuous years. During that time, I remember a good friend said to me, "You guys fight a lot, but you grow from it." One could also grow from ingesting four thousand pancakes in a week, but that doesn't mean it's healthy, and frankly, I don't recommend it. If you find yourselves always in that cycle of fighting and making up, it might be time to consider whether he's right for you. When I was dating Mr. Richter Scale, I thought he was the most exciting man with whom I could ever hope to be. My fabulously wise and fantastic English professor,

Maxine, told me that when I got bored of all the intensity, I'd wise up and find myself a mensch—a purely good man who treated me right. And, as I hope this book has convinced you, there are a lot of mensches out there.

That said, every couple fights now and then. Here's what to bear in mind during those heinous times:

- **Don't let the actual fight go onandonandonandon.** And by "the actual fight" I mean the screaming, face-to-face (or over-the-phone) confrontation part. Usually, both parties say what they need to say in the first five minutes (namely: "You're wrong." "No, you are."). Anything that either of you says after that point will just be repetitive, unkind, and counterproductive. Part ways—even if it's just for half an hour.

- **Get a freaking grip.** Okay, so you were feuding in his apartment, you walked out and slammed the door behind you. You could do what my sister and I did whenever we got sent to our rooms as little girls—open that door and slam it again three or four times, just for emphasis. Or you could cool off. Walk around the block, go for a jog, grab a latte in your local coffee shop and flip through *US Weekly.* Don't call him or any of your friends right away. Just breathe, relax, and remind yourself: a fight is not a breakup. Once you've calmed down, call a friend and tell her what transpired.

- **Don't rush to action.** Each time one of us is fighting with a boyfriend, my friends and I ask each other, "Should I call him? I've already called twice and he's ignored me. But should I call him again?" The answer is always "Wait." Not to be gamesy (although it can't hurt), but because an action can always be postponed—you can always call him tomorrow, when you're not fuming, instead of today, when you are—but it can never be undone. If you call him screaming, you might regret it after you've had some time to think things over.

- **Get a stand-in for when you want to call or e-mail him.** Yes, I realize that sometimes, especially when you're fighting, you feel like you're going to die if you can't talk to him *right now.* Isn't it fun how dating lets us experience adolescence all over again? But we're adults now (boo), and we know that instant gratification can often lead to disappointment in the long run. An easy, if dorky, way to remedy this is to do what my friend Karin and I sometimes do: write him a long e-mail, pour your guts out, get angry, get mean, and then send it—to your best girlfriend. That way you get the satisfaction of getting your feelings off your chest without having to write another long (apologetic) e-mail a few days later.

- **Make a pro and con list.** Sometimes just putting all your reasons for being mad down on paper can help you sort out how you're feeling and what to do about it. Fold a sheet of paper in half, and on one side write all of the good things about your relationship. On the other side, write everything about him that bugs the crap out of you. Of course, if you needed four extra sheets to complete the cons part of your list, that might tell you something. But more likely, you'll see that your relationship—like all normal relationships—is a balance of good and bad elements. And hopefully there's a little bit more good than bad.

- **Give yourself a wallowing time limit.** For as long as you are fighting, each time the phone rings, you will most likely get that hopeful flutter that turns to rage and embarrassment when you realize that it's your grandmother calling, not him. Read Dorothy Parker's short story "A Telephone Call"—which opens with the line "Please, God, let him telephone me now. Dear God, let him call me now. I won't ask anything else of you, truly I won't . . ."—and you'll see that this is not a new phenomenon. However, you are an independent woman with things to do. If you try to stop yourself from wallowing, you'll just keep doing it. Instead, designate a half hour in the morning (don't do it at night, or you'll be tempted to stay up analyzing until four a.m.) when you just allow yourself to obsess about him. When the half hour is up, move on with your day. Talk to friends, but not about him. Go to work and actually work, rather than willing him to e-mail you. Know that either he will contact you today, or you will get to have another self-indulgent pity-party tomorrow morning.

- **Keep it about the issue at hand.** Once you do hear from him or decide to give him a call, there will very often be a second fight—shorter than the original, but often more intense. Sort of like the grand finale at the end of a fireworks display. In the time you've spent apart (it might have been an hour or a week, depending on how mad and stubborn you both were) you've each had a lot of solitary hours to build up resentments, and now you're ready to unleash them. But if your fight was about how he's always late, don't start railing on about how you hate the way he lets his mother boss him around. Stick to solving the issue at hand.

- **Don't blame yourself.** Over the years, each time I've had a fight with a man and started regretting what I said/did/threw, my friends have reminded me that there are two sides to every conflict. Don't beat yourself up, or decide to take all the blame just to smooth things over. Make sure that each of you understands (or at least tries to understand) the other's view. And don't be afraid to fight—it is sometimes the only way for two people to gain common ground on an issue, and a certain amount of it is healthy, I swear.

- **Apologize if you're to blame.** You're a smart woman. You know when you are wrong. And it's okay to say so. In fact, apologizing, though a little bit humbling for most of us, can also feel good. You're taking the high road, and taking responsibility for your actions. If he's half the guy you think he is, he will appreciate your concession and say he's sorry, too.

- **Be kind.** Above all else, be nice to the guy. This one probably sounds a bit obvious—*Oh really, Courtney? We should be nice to our boyfriends?*—but I am astounded by just how nasty people sometimes get in the name of love. Would you ever leave your best friend sitting alone in a restaurant, while you stormed out into the parking lot and drove off? No. Would you even dream of hanging up on a coworker if he said something that annoyed you? I doubt it. Just because your man is yours, you still need to treat him with kindness. In fact, because he's yours, there's even more reason to be kind. Not that you won't want to rip his face off on occasion, but try to remember that he is human and should be treated with the same understanding, kindness, and patience that you give to every other person in your life.

### If One of Your Careers Is Progressing Faster Than the Other's

A friend of mine was applying to med school two summers ago, and so was her live-in boyfriend. When she got into NYU and he was rejected, he started sleeping on the couch. "Men!" we said. "Now if *he* were the more successful one, she'd just be proud of him. She wouldn't measure her own worth against his." Later, when each of them was applying for first residencies, she ended up with a so-so position at a good hospital. He ended up with a plum job at the most prestigious medical center in the country. Was she proud of him? If so, she showed it by moving out and staying at my apartment for a month. Welcome to the new millennium, girls. Step right up. Now that you know how to get rid of the losers and find quality men, there's a whole new set of issues to face. When you're dating someone who is beneath you in terms of money, intelligence, and ambition, you get to be the star. You're promoted every year, while he's still trying to get his band's demo tape recorded. But when you date a man who is as ambitious as you are, it can begin to feel competitive, even if you're not in the same field. Here's how to cope:

- **Leave work at work.** Of course you're going to talk about your jobs, but don't let your jobs be the *only* thing you talk about. These days, many of us spend so much time at our desks that it can be hard to shut off that part of our brains at day's end. If you find yourself in this position, set an actual time limit on how long each of you is allowed to talk about work each night—and then move on to other topics.

- **Blame the system.** Sexism is still rampant in the workplace, no matter what your field, no matter what your level. The fact that your boyfriend probably benefits from this as a professional man might make you want to set fire to his office. Down, girl. A friend of a friend recently told this shocking story over dinner: She and her boyfriend were hired by the same company on the same day to do the same job. She had a master's degree and two years' experience. He had only a bachelor's and had been working in the field for less than six months. One night they were discussing their paychecks, and it came to light that he was making $1,000 more than she each month. When a higher-up position became available, he was the one who got promoted. So how the hell are we supposed to deal with the unfair advantages given to men in the workplace, while still attempting to carry on romantic relationships with them? By realizing that our individual partners are not responsible for the whole mess. That said, if he can't acknowledge that unfair sex-based discrepancies exist in the workplace, you might want to slip a little Gloria Steinem onto his nightstand, where Harry Potter usually resides.

- **Lie to him.** This is pretty much the only context in which I think it is advisable to lie to your man: if he's just gotten a huge promotion or a great new high-paying job and you find yourself feeling uneasy or jealous or angry about it, then you'd better put on a big fake smile and act happy anyway. Because the truth is, you *should* be happy for him and proud of him, too. Any negative feelings you have—be they because you wish *you* had been promoted, or because you know that this new job will infringe on the amount of time he spends with you—are probably selfish ones. Not that you can't talk to him about them eventually, but your initial reaction to his good news should not be "Oh crap."

- **Stand up for yourself.** Just as you should be positive and excited when good things happen for him at work, he should be equally supportive of your career. Despite all the advances women have made, it is still difficult for some men to deal with their girlfriends' success. If your man is one of them, he will have to be trained out of it. If you are both serious about your relationship, then it's important to recognize that you will not always be on the same footing. Throughout your dating life and marriage, sometimes you'll be up when he's down—in terms of work, health, friends, family, and everything that matters—and vice versa. Acting sympathetic when someone is feeling miserable is pretty easy. But it takes strength and selflessness to be genuinely happy for someone else—especially someone you love. Practice this, and demand that your man do the same.

## If Your Friends Can't Stand Him

I met my ex—a tall, handsome, foreign artist with an irresistible accent—and fell instantly in love with him, during a quiet August in Manhattan when every single one of my good friends was away on vacation. In fact, it seemed as though the two of us were the only people in the city that month. We walked through Central Park talking for hours. We read the *Times* in little outdoor cafés. We saw indie films at the Angelika, and sipped champagne at the Carlyle. We were a freaking month-long movie montage with a Frank Sinatra song playing in the background. I e-mailed my friends, who were traveling through Europe or sunning themselves in the Hamptons. I told them that we had already discussed getting married. Most of them replied that they were excited to meet him when they returned. Karin, the relationship voice of reason, was in Nice, but managed to send a one-liner: "Can't write much. But don't do *anything* until I get back."

As soon as I introduced him to my friends, I realized that they were not going to fall instantly in love. "He's a little old," one of them said. "Actually, he's ancient," said another.

It was true. He was twelve years my senior, though that hadn't seemed to matter when it was just the two of us.

"Is he seriously a painter?" someone asked. "Have you ever seen his studio?"

I had, and if owning paint and canvases makes someone a painter, then he was one. But if that someone actually needs to paint something, well then, he wasn't keeping up his end of the deal. In truth, he came from money and didn't need to support himself. The art was more of a hobby than anything else.

"Let's say the two of you do get married," another friend asked. "Is he going to expect you to leave the country and move home with him?"

"Certainly not," I said, though we had never discussed it.

What I realized when my friends returned to New York (other than the fact that they are a bossy, critical lot) was that I was thinking with my heart, not my head. Your friends love you, and know you deserve the best. In most cases, if they are bold enough to strongly object to someone whom you are dating (even if you happen to think he's the bee's knees), there's probably a reason. If you want to try to make it work, both with him and with them:

- **Force interaction.** Set up small group outings, or invite friends over for dinner with you and your man one at a time. Perhaps if they interact with him a bit more, they'll start to see what you like about him. Or, on the other hand, you might realize the truth behind what they've been saying. This sort of forced interaction can be stressful. Just remember that everyone there has one thing in common—they all care about you. Take a deep breath, add cheap wine, and stir.

- **Ask them to list their complaints.** Instead of letting them make negative remarks here and there, or demanding that they stop criticizing your man altogether, ask your friends to tell you all their hesitations at once—either face-to-face or (even better) on paper. Then . . .

- **Weigh what they've said and assess whether it has merit.** You have a good head on your shoulders, even if it sometimes floats off to a faraway place called Loveland. When my friends started pointing out the flaws in my man, I knew that they were right. You should be able to recognize when your friends have a point, and act accordingly. On the other hand, you should also know when to tell them to mind their own beeswax. One of my best friends was seeing a guy for two years, and I thought he was just wrong for her. I held my tongue until he started a fight and broke up with her on her birthday (they got back together the next day), at which point I sent her a novella-length e-mail about how much he sucked. She let me know that, although she appreciated my concern, she had chosen to be with him despite his flaws, and she did not need any help from me in determining her feelings for him. She was right. It wasn't my place. Insert foot in mouth. Two years later, they're still together, and I've really come to like him. When balancing a relationship and friends, there are a lot of opinions being cast—the most important one is your own.

- **Don't tell him what they're saying.** Sometimes a guy can just tell when his girlfriend's friends don't like him. But your friends are probably discreet enough that he has no idea. Keep it that way. Don't vent to him about the problem. It will only make him feel bad and lead to more animosity.

## If He Loves You, but He Seems to Care More about Work (or Family, or His Car, or His Fantasy Baseball Team) than He Does about You

When you're apart, you think of him all day long. It's not like you're sitting home eating bonbons and have nothing better to do. You are busy with your career, your friends, your life. And yet, as you work on a major project, you might happen to glance up at your computer clock, notice that it's noon, and start wondering what he's having for lunch. *A salad? Pizza? A bologna sandwich? Wait, does he even like bologna?* Or, as you collate yet another four hundred pages for your boss, you might get distracted by the memory of a trip you took to the beach together last summer. You'll recall how he told you that when he was a kid, his parents used to always set up a volleyball net in the sand and they'd have a family match. *Hey, maybe this July, in Nantucket, you should talk to his mom about re-creating that as a surprise. You can rent the net and ball, set it up while he's still sleeping* . . . No matter how busy things get at the office, you always find time to send him a quick e-mail and think about how he's doing. In fact, if you tried to spend the whole day not thinking about him, you would probably fail.

Sorry I have to break this news to you, but your boyfriend is most likely *not* the same way. He's just doing his work, checking out his team's score on ESPN.com, joking around with his officemates. When he sees you later that night, he will be thrilled to spend time with you—but until then, you're not consuming his thoughts. Which isn't to say that he loves you any less than you love him, or that he's an uncaring Neanderthal. Men have an annoying tendency to compartmentalize. And as a woman, you might (especially in recent years, thanks to a book we will not name) have an equally annoying tendency to assume that because a guy is busy, he is clearly just not that into you. Relax.

## If He Hits You

I believe in giving an otherwise good guy the benefit of the doubt if he messes up. He forgot your birthday? Well, that was a stupid mistake. He ran your car into a stop sign because he was trying to find a Van Morrison tape under the passenger seat? That's annoying, but it's just an unfortunate accident. However, physical abuse is not a mess up, or a stupid mistake, or just an accident. *Abuse cannot be excused for any reason.* Period. I don't care if you've been together six years and he was an absolute prince right up until the day he slapped you. I don't care if his mother is in the hospital, or his boss is putting pressure on him, or if he swears that it will never, ever happen again. As intelligent women who want to date up, we've sworn off all classes of loser—and a man who hits a woman (or punches her, or kicks her, or grabs her wrist a little too hard, or forces her to have sex when she doesn't want to, or verbally assaults and demeans her) is pretty much the most despicable sort of man I can think of. I spent a year volunteering in a domestic violence shelter in Boston. There, women from all economic backgrounds and their children were seeking refuge from batterers—men whom they had once dated and married, and whom they often still loved. When you have a mortgage and a family to think about, it can be difficult if not impossible to walk away from an abusive relationship.

If your boyfriend becomes abusive in any way, it may seem too hard to leave—you love him, depend on him, need him. However, any man who would hit you once is very likely to do it again. Don't stay with someone who endangers you. If it seems hard to walk away now, think of how difficult it will be when you have children together. There is so much gray area in relationships—cheating, lying, fighting, all of these things can be deal-breakers. Or not. But when it comes to physical or emotional violence, it's very simple—please, please leave.

At the risk of sounding like an after-school special, if you find yourself in an abusive relationship there is help: the National Domestic Violence Hotline (1-800-799-SAFE) is confidential, and you can call and speak with someone twenty-four hours a day.

# Marrying Up

"Marriage is not a ritual or an end. It is a long, intricate, intimate dance together and nothing matters more than your own sense of balance and your choice of partner."

—Amy Bloom

If there's one lesson about dating that I hope you've learned from this book, it's to proceed slowly in all your romantic endeavors. Take your time getting to know him, don't rush into labeling the relationship too quickly, and don't have sex right away. It is even more essential to go slowly when you are considering moving in together and getting married. Selecting a husband is the most important choice you will make in your life—don't be swayed by what your friends are doing, or by where others (i.e., your mother) think you ought to be. Instead, remember that in romance, as in all other endeavors, the most important voice to listen to is your own.

This chapter provides a guide for getting to "I do" without threats, fights, or ultimatums. If you've followed my advice so far and truly found a man who is your equal, then the rest will come in its due time. Be patient.

## Living Together

Just because you love spending time with your boyfriend, and enjoy sleepovers at one another's places, doesn't necessarily mean you should move in together. Nor does the fact that both of your roommates just bailed, or that you're tired of paying $900 in rent every month. Moving in together is a precursor to marriage, plain and simple. You should do it only if an engagement has already occurred or is looming in the very near future. Why? Because too much emotional damage is at stake if you decide it's not right. Think of how devastating it is when you break up with someone whom you love. Then add to that the need to find a new place, move all your belongings, and decide who gets to keep the DVD player. Not a pleasant thought. You can always wait six months, and then move in together. It's a lot harder to move in, realize it was a mistake, and still keep your relationship alive.

Here's how to assess whether or not you're ready.

**You're on the same page about finances.** Money is perhaps the most important issue in any relationship, but if your man is wealthy, it's even more essential that you agree on how to spend your cash. You don't want to wait until after you're living under the same roof to find out that you've been saving since kindergarten, while he's chosen to invest in four Jaguars instead of a 401(k). Plan ahead how you will divide the monthly bills and rent—will you split everything down the middle, or will whichever one of you makes more contribute a higher percentage? Consider even the smallest expenses, such as groceries, toilet paper, and magazine subscriptions. Do you want to create a joint bank account in addition to your own individual accounts? Do you each have a realistic sense of how much the other makes (yes, you should know the exact figure) and what the other's spending habits are?

**You've talked very seriously about getting married.** Again, living together without knowing that he intends to marry you is just silly. It's like showing up to a job every day even though no one's paying you and you don't actually work there. Men are very literal, so don't take his desire to live with you as his unspoken intention to marry you. Ask him flat out how much longer he plans to wait, and tell him that, to you, living together signifies a promise of engagement. One note: never, ever, ever move in together to try to resuscitate a dying relationship. Things should be better than they've ever been to start out, because living together is hard work.

**You're comfortable with his major lifestyle choices.** A good friend of mine had been dating a young college professor for three years. They got along well, he treated her like gold, and he had a beautiful four-bedroom house. So when he asked her to move in, she automatically accepted. The only problem was that, despite the fact that he had left high school about fifteen years earlier, he still smoked a lot of pot. This bothered my friend from the start, but once she moved in, it started to consume her, and eventually led her to move out. You should feel comfortable in your own house (and your own relationship!) and so should he. If there is a major lifestyle issue on which you differ (drinking, drugs, the desire to have children . . .) don't assume that the magic of moving in together is going to make it go away. Deal with it beforehand, and if you can't deal with it, find someone else.

**You like his friends and he likes yours.** You don't have to be best buds, but look at it this way—you know that cigar-and-beer-filled Friday-night poker game he's always hosting? Well now it'll be happening right in your living room. Are you comfortable having his friends over? And are you comfortable spending time with your own friends in your man's presence?

**Your families are on board.** This one might seem antiquated. Why should you give up the chance to wake up in each other's arms every morning just because his—or your own—mother thinks it's a bad idea? Because if you are serious about marriage, you will be joining your lives—and your two families—together in the very near future. Better to have everyone excited about the relationship than to cast scandal on it from the start. You'll be married soon enough—and then you'll be longing to have that big bed all to yourself again anyway.

**You're willing to give up ever living alone (or with your friends) again.** Think long and hard about the sacrifices involved in sharing space with your man. If things go according to plan, you'll be living with him for the rest of your life. You might feel ready to live with him, but not ready to give up your freedom. That's okay. Take all the time you need, and when it's right, you'll know.

**You've discussed how you'll handle household duties.** My father always says that one of the first things my mother told him after they got engaged was, "I don't do laundry, and I don't do windows." I probably don't have to tell you that she is the smartest woman I know. Make sure that each of you knows ahead of time what you expect of the other in terms of cooking, cleaning, yard work, and so on. Ridiculous as it seems, some men still think that moving in with a woman is their domestic get-out-of-jail-free card. If you're not planning to cook or clean, tell him. If you're anal and he resembles Pig Pen, a chores chart might be in order. If neither of you wants to clean, hire a service. Why ruin an otherwise great relationship by fighting over a dirty pile of laundry and some crusty dishes?

## Once You Decide to Cohabitate

The decision to move in together is a big one. But let's say you are both ready. What next? I've known plenty of couples who have moved in together and ended up married. And I've also known a few who didn't make it long enough to get their security deposit back. Here are some things to bear in mind if you want to make it last.

**Get a new (and neutral) space.** Last winter my friend Gretchen moved into her boyfriend Lucas's condo. Because he owned and she rented, they both thought it best for her to move in to his place. But, perhaps because he'd spent so much time alone there, Lucas was never able to share the space. His bathroom and closet and cabinets never made the leap to becoming *their* bathroom and closet and cabinets. I grant that Lucas is a bit more high-maintenance than most men. You may think that your boyfriend wouldn't even notice if you dumped out the contents of his dresser and packed it full of your own clothes. Still, the best location is a new location—an apartment or house that neither of you previously lived in, where you can start your life together from scratch. If it's impossible for you to do this right away because of a lease or mortgage payments, at least think of it as a goal for the near future.

**Keep seeing your friends.** Many women move in with their boyfriends and suddenly they might as well be pictured on the side of a milk carton, so much have they vanished from their former social circle. Don't be one of them. Friends are still essential, and it's important to make sure yours know that just because you now live with your boyfriend, you still value them. It's also healthy for your relationship with your man if you are not always readily available to hang out on the couch with him. Remember how breezy you were back when you started dating? It's good to keep a bit of that mystery and longing between the two of you, whether you've been together for thirty days or thirty years.

**Don't worry when the living together honeymoon is over.** The other day at work, I was in the elevator with two editors whom I don't know, but of course I eavesdropped on their conversation anyway. One was complaining to the other, "When we moved in together three months ago, it was like a twenty-four-hour party. He'd make martinis every night, we'd get drunk, we'd laugh, we had tons of sex, we never wanted to leave the apartment. What happened to us?" The other woman (who I then noticed was wearing a wedding ring) laughed: "Real life happened, honey," she said. Just like when you started dating and you thought he was the best thing ever (only to learn a few weeks later that though you love him, he has his flaws), when you first move in together, of course it will be entirely fun and carefree. But remember: when the initial butterflies stage of your relationship ended and you came to see him for who he is, things only got better and deeper between you. And so it will be when you live together. That said . . .

**Go on dates.** I lived with a former boyfriend for a few months, and after the initial euphoric stage passed, things got, well, boring. I'd wake up in the middle of the night, and instead of wanting to make out like I used to, I'd tap his shoulder, and ask, "Did you buy milk?" He would call me at work during the day, but not just to say "I love you," like he used to. Instead he'd say "Did you turn the coffee maker off this morning?" or "How much do we owe the cable company?" If this sounds like you, get thyself out of that rut—STAT. You're not even married yet. You have no children, no real joint responsibilities. Successful relationships take effort. If it seems that all you can talk about is whether or not to buy new curtains, jump-start your love life. Dedicate yourselves to going on at least one real date every week, no matter how busy you are. This is a good habit to get into for the future, and will remind you why you wanted to live together in the first place.

**Divvy up the chores.** When you live with a roommate, in most cases you split the chores down the middle—sometimes you take out the garbage, sometimes she does. Sometimes you do the dishes, sometimes she does. When you live with a significant other, the situation can be a bit less egalitarian, and this is a good thing—as long as one of you isn't doing all the work. When I lived with my ex, I'd cook dinner every night and he would do the dishes. I love cooking and loathe cleaning, and he was the opposite, so this was an ideal situation for both of us. In addition, I don't mind cleaning a bathroom every now and then, and he knew his way around a vacuum and a lawn mower. Living with your boyfriend versus a friend or roommate offers the chance to do the chores that you prefer. But make sure you're both contributing equally (whatever that means to you).

**Find a room of one's own.** When my friend Kathleen insisted on moving into a two-bedroom London flat with her boyfriend Ivan, none of our friends could understand why. Sure, it's great to have a guest room, but the expense seemed extravagant. Then one night she told me a secret—the second bedroom was hers, and she had told Ivan that she would never consider living with him without it. Though she doesn't sleep in that room very often, Kathleen says it's essential to know that one part of their home is only hers. Financially, you may not be able to get a whole room. But make sure there is a space in your joint dwelling that reflects exactly who you are as an individual—a space where you can go and close the door whenever you need a quiet spot to work, or think, or just eat a bowl of ice cream in peace. Again, this will become essential when you get married and have children, so start now. And speaking of children . . .

**Don't turn momsy.** Some women fall prey to this ugly condition as soon as they get a boyfriend, but most remain immune until they are living under the same roof with a guy who can't pick up his socks, or who feels the need to shake off like a wet Labrador the moment he steps out of the shower. Resist! For the sake of your relationship, if not your sanity, don't pick up after him, nag him, or baby him. Either learn to live with his occasional childlike ways, or tell him in no uncertain terms to change them.

**Don't get a dog for at least six months.** This one may seem weird, but it's from the very convincing psychological school known as Live and Learn. For some reason, a lot of live-in couples I know get a dog before they even get silverware. I guess the reasoning is that if they're ready to make a commitment to each other, they're ready to commit to a pet. Not so. The first six months of living together will be a big adjustment. Get used to each other before you add a four-legged player into the mix. And make sure the situation is for good—otherwise, you'll end up having to negotiate joint custody of a beagle with a guy you'd rather never see again.

## Getting the Ring on Your Finger

I've been proposed to twice, but I've never been engaged. I always pictured that when it was time for the right guy to ask, it would be like a scene from the best romantic movie ever. Jen and Karl, my first close friends to get engaged, made this seem all the more likely when they arrived at a party after a snowy evening walk in Central Park and announced that they had just decided to get married. They had been together for three years, and of course they talked about marriage, but the proposal was a surprise and that night Jen looked like the happiest woman alive.

However, in my research for this book, I interviewed dozens of newly married and engaged women, and I asked each one of them if her proposal was unexpected. The overwhelming majority said no, and that in fact, to sum it up in one woman's words: "I was practically holding a gun to his head for six months before he got it together to ask."

This struck me as not only utterly unromantic, but also sad. And it made me wonder—are ultimatums (or death threats, for that matter) necessary? Do they work? I took these questions to the best team of experts I know: my mother and my aunts. All of them long and happily married, they agreed that this is the way to do it if you want your marriage to last:

**Follow the same guidelines as when you decided to live together.** You shouldn't even be thinking about marrying someone before you know whether you're on the same page about major issues like finances, children, career, and religion. And (although this statement is not endorsed by my mom and aunts) I personally think it's essential to live together for at least six months before you get married. Dating a man, even very seriously, can never replicate what it's like to share your space with him.

**Keep the lines of communication open.** One woman I know admits to putting the Tiffany's catalog on the kitchen table, open to a photo of her dream ring, in hopes that it will spark inspiration in her man's mind while he's drinking his morning coffee. This is not the way to talk to your boyfriend about marriage. After you have been dating for six months or so, it's perfectly acceptable to tell him what you expect in terms of the future. And you can be specific—if you want to be married within two years, say so. If you plan to start having kids at thirty, tell him. A proposal should be something you've discussed together, evaluated, and agreed upon as the best next step. The culture of movie romance that we have been raised in makes a lot of us think that love should be spontaneous and effortless. This is just plain dumb. As educated and ambitious women, we know that everything worth having in our professional lives comes at a certain cost—If you want that big promotion, you'll be spending a lot of quality time in your office on Saturdays—and the world of relationships is no different. An engagement is not just your ticket to a Vera Wang gown and one hell of a party. Deciding whom to marry is the most serious and important decision you'll ever make. You'll be successful if you're both open and honest about how you expect things to proceed, and if you treat the process as you should—with happiness and love, but also a clear head, the knowledge that marriage is hard work, and a sense of what's best for you both. To that end . . .

**Make sure you're doing this because it is the right time for you, not because of outside pressure.** Many of us hit a point where we look up one day and all of our friends are coupling off, getting engaged, and purchasing homes. And when this happens, even though we never expected to be That Girl, suddenly we start to freak out. When my first close friend from childhood got engaged, I panicked. I remember going on a date that night—a ho-hum second date with a so-so tax attorney—and thinking, *Sure. This one will do. I'll just marry him and that will be that.* One of the hardest parts of being an independent woman in the world of modern dating is learning that every one of us makes our own choices—about school, jobs, men—in our own time. A friend of mine just moved in with her boyfriend and got engaged after only a few months of dating. This sent every other woman we know into a complete and total tizzy. What the hell was wrong with this girl? They all raged about how she was rushing in, panicked about her split decision. But it seemed to me that there were other questions looming—why were their own (much longer) relationships not progressing as quickly? Why hadn't their boyfriends popped the question yet? What the hell was wrong with them? Don't stress about what everyone else is doing. Just be true to yourself and your relationship, and let things unfold naturally. That said . . .

**Think of marriage like buying a house.** My college friends hate this analogy, which I came up with freshman year. But I still think it's apt and worth remembering. At any given moment, in any given place, there are X amount of people looking to buy houses. When you find yourself in need of a house, you buy the best one you can afford and move in. You buy a house when you need a house. You don't live in a cardboard box for twelve years until the absolute perfect home becomes available. Likewise, if you met the perfect man for you at the age of ten, chances are you would not marry him on the spot. You should never settle. But marriage, like buying a house, is all about timing. When you're ready, you'll marry the best man you can find who is also ready. If you think your man is perfect for you in all ways, but he just doesn't want to get married yet, then he is not perfect for you.

**Say goodbye to Miss Independent.** No, I don't mean that you have to throw away your Kelly Clarkson CDs. But you are going to have to part with some of your hard-earned independence if you want to get married. You should discuss ahead of time how you will handle situations that occur for one of you, but affect you both. The most common of these is relocation for a job—if he gets a career opportunity across the country and he can't pass it up, are you willing to trade in your own job and life to go with him? And what if the reverse happened—could he drop everything for you? The only downside to dating up is that because both of you are fully invested in your careers, you might butt heads when it comes to decisions like this. Discuss how you'll handle them ahead of time, so there won't be any surprises down the road.

**Ultimatums don't work.** Clearly, I am a girl who believes in dating rules. You should never pay on a date. You should absolutely never sleep with a man after seeing him only once or twice. You shouldn't call your boyfriend more often than he calls you. I believe in these rules because they work—if you follow them, you will be instantly more attractive and interesting to men. Unfortunately, there are no hard and fast rules for how to make someone propose. This seems totally logical and healthy to me. Being a little bit breezy early on in a relationship gives your man time to get to know the real you (and you him) from a bit of a distance. There is nothing manipulative or inappropriate about that. But there's something wrong with trying to convince a man to marry you—by threats, ultimatums, guilt, or other means. Do you want a marriage based on any of those things? According to my mom, my father proposed to her after they'd been dating for three weeks. She didn't say yes until much later, but as she put it, "When it's the right guy, you won't even have to think about ultimatums. He'll be so eager to spend the rest of his life with you that he'll be practically bursting at the seams wanting to ask." In a country with a 60 percent divorce rate, new marriages need all the help they can get. Start things off right by telling your man in clear terms what you expect. If he says that he's on the same page, have faith in him and be patient. And if he doesn't come through in a timely fashion, move on.

My friend Sarah dated her ex-boyfriend Jake for four years. When they met, she was thirty, a senior magazine editor who had dated nearly every eligible bachelor in New York. She was ready to settle down.

After just the first couple of dates with Jake, Sarah knew that he was the guy she wanted to marry. They held the same beliefs about religion, family, and politics. They both loved to read and cook, and Jake was the godfather to several of his nieces and nephews. He adored children, which was great, because Sarah wanted four of them.

Things progressed quickly, and after just eight months, she gave him her bottom line—she wanted to be married within the year and start raising a family. Jake said he felt exactly the same way. From then on, each time they spent a long weekend in the country, or went out to a nice restaurant for dinner, we all expected Sarah to return with a big fat diamond on her hand.

A year went by, and then a year and a half. Finally, Sarah asked him why he hadn't proposed yet. First it was that they hadn't been together long enough. Six months later, he said he had almost done it, but got cold feet. Three months after that, he said he was ready, and finally popped the question—but he refused to tell anyone about the engagement and suggested that they hold off on planning a wedding for a year or two. She knew he was stalling, but didn't see that she had any choice in the matter. "He's the perfect man for me," she kept saying. "He's the only person I want to live my life with." But it had become clear that Jake had no interest in that life.

When they broke up, the phrase Sarah kept repeating was a common, rather heartbreaking one: "I've wasted the best years of my life."

There's something about that statement that irks me. Sarah is beautiful and will still be gorgeous when she is eighty years old. But there is also truth to it—not every thirty-four-year-old woman needs to be married with four kids, but Sarah wanted to be, and by lying and stalling for four years, Jake robbed her of the chance to find someone who could give her that life.

You cannot and should not beg or force someone to propose. But you also must not wait around if your man is stalling and you want a commitment. Don't leave because you want him to chase you. Leave because you can do better—he is not the perfect man for you if he doesn't share your plans for the future. And there is someone out there just itching to get down on bended knee and give you the life you deserve.

## Lord of the Rings

My friend Jen is utterly unmaterialistic and clueless about jewelry. So on that snowy night when she and Karl got engaged, she proudly held forth her ring to all of our friends and exclaimed, "I love it. It's shiny." Later, on the phone to her mother, she described it as, "So pretty! It's silver."

"Actually, it's platinum," Karl whispered.

"And it's shiny! And so pretty!" she said.

Karl, amazing man that he is, just shook his head and laughed. That shiny, pretty thing was a two-carat diamond that had clearly set him back.

Girls like Jen are a rarity. On the other end of the spectrum you have me and my friend Karin, who have known exactly the rings we want since birth. (Note to my future husband: it's the six-prong Tiffany setting in platinum. Moving on . . .) So, although I am not yet engaged myself, I already feel like an expert on the topic of engagement rings. Some things to keep in mind:

**Tell a friend to tell him what you want.** If you're afraid he's going to present you with some honking pink stone, get one of your female friends to tell him that you had your heart set on a small marquise cut. He'll be grateful for the help if she's not too pushy about it.

**Pick out the ring together.** Even better, tell him what you want on your own. Some of my friends find this idea totally unromantic because they want the ring to be a surprise. But the vast majority of couples go ring shopping together these days. Communication will be an essential part of your marriage, so why not start now, by clearly communicating to him exactly what you hope to find inside that little velvet box.

**Family rings.** When you're dealing with men of a certain social status (that is to say, super-rich ones), your chances of being offered an heirloom ring will skyrocket. Very wealthy people often like to keep their prized possessions in the family. Your man should tell you ahead of time if this is the case, not just slip a ring on your finger and say, "It was my grandmother's." That doesn't leave you much room to say, "But it looks like a Ring Pop." If you like the idea of wearing someone else's ring, by all means do. By accepting it, you will be solidifying your bond with his entire family. But if you don't want the ring, say so. They will get over it. I promise.

**Remember the five C's.** It's important for you and your man to familiarize yourselves with these terms before you even set foot in a jewelry store.

1. **Carat.** The weight of the diamond. One carat weighs one-fifth of a gram, or 200 milligrams. Better eat your Wheaties if you're looking for a big rock. A carat is

divided into 100 points, so a diamond that's half a carat is a 50-point diamond. Not that you need to know anything about half carats.

2. **Clarity.** Almost every stone has tiny flaws that occur in nature (called inclusions)—bubbles, cracks, or specks that are usually impossible to see with the naked eye. Clarity is determined by viewing a diamond under a microscope with ten times magnification. The ratings are IF (internally flawless—you can relate), VVS (very very small inclusions), VS (very small inclusions), SI (small inclusions), I1 (inclusions recognizable, but not diminishing brilliance to the naked eye), I2 (large and many inclusions, slightly diminishing brilliance), and I3 (large and many inclusions, diminishing brilliance). All good information to have, even though those last four classifications won't apply to you. Clearly.

3. **Color.** Diamonds range in color from perfectly clear (which is the most desirable, and given a ranking of D) to yellow (which is the least desirable, and ranked as Z). The darker the stone, the more earthy color it picked up before being mined (and this is a bad thing). Some diamonds naturally have a tint of another color (think J-Lo's pink rock from Ben Affleck). These bear the adorable name "Fancies."

4. **Cut.** This is different from the shape. (The most common shapes are round, oval, pear, emerald, and marquise. If you don't know what these look like, get thee to www.tiffany.com immediately.) Cut determines the bril-

liance (or sparkle, to use a totally unscientific word) of the stone, and is considered the most important C. It refers to the series of flat, angled surfaces that occur when a diamond is cut.

5. **Commitment.** No, I'm not talking about the commitment you're making to love, honor, and cherish this man 'til death do you part. I'm talking about the commitment you're making to the one piece of jewelry you will have to wear for the rest of your life. If he proposes and you don't like what you see, it's okay to be honest (but gentle), and tell him you want something different. Most men cannot pick out an appropriate pair of socks, let alone an engagement ring. Help him out, and do not take it as a sign if he has no clue what you want.

## The Big Moment

Relationship milestones are the best. They make all the pain and suffering of dating worthwhile. The first time you introduce him as your boyfriend. The first time you leave your toothbrush at his place. The first time you say "I love you." And of course, no milestone even touches the moment when he proposes. In the last few months, several of my friends have gotten engaged—one on a bike ride along the Golden Gate Bridge, one under fireworks on the Fourth of July, another on a golf course in Hawaii, another on the island of Capri, and another still at her own kitchen table over dinner.

They all describe the event in the same way. "It was the most incredible time of my life. And I don't remember it at all."

When your engagement moment arrives, revel in it. Soon will come a flurry of dress fittings and heated debates about centerpieces and the merits of chicken versus beef, or chocolate wedding cake versus angel food (umm, hello, people, chocolate). But before all that begins, take a moment to look back at the long dating career you've had. All the schlumps and disappointments and heartache. Perhaps, like many of my friends have, you might find yourself saying good-bye to memories of your exes (one woman I know started dreaming about her former boyfriends when she got engaged). Just as you've worked hard to get where you are in your job, you have worked toward this moment—and the reward is all thanks to you and your smart decisions. If you've followed the advice in this book and truly dated up, you have a long and happy marriage ahead of you. A marriage that will include all of the essential elements for happiness:

- **Mutual respect and admiration.** You searched for a man who was your absolute equal—whose career ambitions and goals were similar to your own, and who understood your passions. Now you can look forward to being proud of him for a lifetime, and to having a partner who's proud of you.

- **Financial compatibility.** Thank God you didn't marry the starving artist in the flannel shirt whom you once considered the love of your life. Much like a fish and a bird, a starving artist and a career girl might love each other—but where would they live? It is my hope that by now, any guilt you had about admitting that money matters has vanished. By acknowledging the vital role that finances play in a happy marriage, you have saved yourself years of aggravation and frustration.

- **Shared ideals and a vision of the future.** Perhaps the only thing weirder than the day your first friend gets married is the day your first friend gets divorced. Sadly, a friend of mine ended her marriage recently, after only two years. When I asked her what had gone wrong, she said simply, "We thought just loving each other was enough. We never asked each other the hard questions." If you have discussed the importance of major life issues—money, career, family, religion—you are already a step ahead of the pack.

- **The know-how to handle tough times.** Relationships are not all sunshine and daffodils, as anyone who has been in one knows. But because you know the right ways to fight, and how to honestly address what is important to you, your marriage will be all the stronger.

- **Friendship.** A dating up woman doesn't end up with someone just because she is infatuated. She chooses the partner who is just that—a partner. An equal. A friend.

- **Love.** Equality and financial wisdom are essential parts of a strong marriage. But the most central element is always love. I don't believe that love can exist without respect and understanding. Because you've dated up and asserted what you want from a man instead of playing games and waiting for magic, you have found your way to the love of your life.

# Marrying Up

When I finished writing the first draft of this book, I boarded a train from Manhattan to Boston one morning with the full manuscript in my hand. I sat beside a beautiful woman in her sixties dressed in a perfect green suit.

"Are you an editor?" she asked me, gesturing toward the pages in my lap.

"No," I told her. "A writer."

"Is it a novel?" she asked.

"Nope," I said. "It's a dating book."

And so we spent a good hour talking about the importance of dating up.

She was a doctor married to a doctor, and she summed it up better than I had to that point. "Marrying your financial equal is so important. But it's not just about money," she said. "It's about the life that you will live together. When a woman becomes serious about marriage, she needs to move beyond the men she's been seeing and learn to date—and marry—up."

She told me about attending medical school at a time when the class was about 95 percent male, and about falling in love with one of the few men there who realized that her career was going to be as essential and demanding as his own.

"We had two children, and it was important to us both to take care of them without outside help," she told me. "I worked days, he worked nights. Knowing that my husband understood how important my career was, was what saw me through those early years. When you're a doctor, you have a dedication to your job—just because your shift is officially over doesn't mean you go home if there are patients waiting to be seen. My husband always understood this about me, and I understood it about him. I think if I had married a teacher or a lawyer, he would have understood, too. It's all about finding someone with the same level of passion for his job and his life that you have for yours."

I sat back, taking in what she had said. It was exactly what I wanted this book to convey.

An hour or so later, the train passed through some beautiful seaside town, with private sailboats docked in front of huge waterfront homes. "Do you know where we are?" My seatmate asked.

I shook my head.

"Wherever it is," she said. "I'd say that the girls married up."

# The Ten Tenets of Dating Up

"Love is everything it's cracked up to be."

—Erica Jong

This book is meant to see you through a great relationship—from meeting a quality man to hearing him say "I do." But sometimes there are starts and stops, or questions that arise as you go. While I hope you'll follow the advice I give, I don't really expect you to re-read the whole thing every time you meet a new prospect or have to have brunch with your boyfriend's mom. When I was interviewing women for these chapters, a lot of them seemed to view dating as similar to reading a Dostoevsky novel—fascinating and enjoyable, if only they had the Cliff's Notes. Well, ladies, here you go.

Turn to this shorthand guide whenever you need assistance, and you'll be well on your way to dating up.

1. **Realize that you're worth it.** The first step in becoming a dating up woman is realizing that you deserve a man who is every bit as ambitious, intelligent, financially mature, and willing to love as you are. Once you know that in your heart, it's much easier to . . .

2. **Leave the schlumps behind.** You can't hope to find Mr. Right but continue to see Mr. Not-on-Your-Life. It doesn't matter how cute he is, how much potential he has, or how close his rock band is to signing their first record contract. You have to take a man for who he is, not who he might be in the future. Promise yourself that you will see only worthy men from here on out—even if it means that you spend a month or two without going on a date.

3. **Admit that money matters.** Female empowerment is meant to empower us, not leave us broke from going dutch. You can afford dinner out any night of the week—but it's nice to know that your boyfriend can as well, and that he's gentlemanly enough to want to pay for you. Financial security is a key part of a successful marriage, so do yourself a favor and seek out only men who meet your monetary needs from the start.

4. **Know there's more where he came from.** Women are far more in danger of getting hung up on some guy who they think is The One than they are of actually letting The One pass them by. When you're out there meeting

men, remember that there are plenty of great guys in the world. No matter how good someone looks on paper, no matter how much money he has, the most important thing is how he treats you. If a man isn't showing you the respect and admiration you deserve right from the start, forget about him—there are better ones out there. I swear.

5. **Hold back in the beginning.** When we meet someone great, a lot of us dive right into relationship mode. But if you want the relationship to last, resist this urge. Imagine the slowest possible speed at which you'd like to proceed, and then go twice as slow as that. In the beginning, don't divulge a lot of overly personal information, don't act clingy, don't call him to make plans, and don't sleep with him.

6. **Be patient.** Many of us live for those relationship state-of-the-union conversations, but they have to come in their own due time. Remember that the most important thing at any given moment is how your man treats you. Let him be the one to initiate all of the milestones, such as when you are officially a couple, when you say "I love you" for the first time, and when you start talking about moving in together. A woman who dates up would never dream of giving her man an ultimatum—because ultimatums have no place in a relationship that is built on mutual trust and respect.

7. **Be yourself.** Though it's important to be breezy in those first few months, don't pretend to be someone you're

not. It's completely possible to be yourself while still creating emotional distance. The objective here is to find the man who best complements you—the real you, not some watered-down, man-pleasing version of you.

8. **Be kind.** Once you are in a relationship, remember to treat your man with the same kindness you expect from him and that you extended to him in the beginning. All too often, women spend years looking for a great guy, and once they find him, they start nagging and complaining and trying to change him. It's healthy to fight every now and then, but pick your battles. Just because he's yours doesn't mean you shouldn't be nice to him. In fact, because he's yours you have all the more reason to want to make his life happy and pleasant.

9. **Have faith.** Relationships are hard work. There are plenty of false starts and near misses on the path to a happy marriage. But remember that everything you've achieved in life so far, personally and professionally, has taken some effort. You're a smart, independent woman, and there *is* a worthy man out there for you. Give him some time to show his face, and while you're waiting . . .

10. **Enjoy it.** At the end of the day, none of us *needs* a man anymore. We have our own incomes and support networks. We have entirely full lives, and very healthy bank accounts. Still, most of us would be more than happy to make room for a great partner. Dating and relationships can be trying, but have fun while you're in the process. Every time I've ever been on a horrible date and then re-

counted the story to my mother, all she can do is laugh, and say "You're young. Enjoy it." You're going to meet a lot of duds before you find Mr. Right. This is the only time in your life that you'll get to meet a variety of interesting men and decide what you do and don't want from your ultimate relationship. Learn to laugh, and realize that each bad date gets you that much closer to meeting the quality man of your dreams.

# About the Author

J. Courtney Sullivan lives in New York City. Her writing has appeared in the *New York Times, Allure, Tango,* and the *New York Observer.*